❧ BRUSH OF AN ANGEL'S WING ❧

Brush of an Angel's Wing

Charlie W. Shedd

Servant Publications
Ann Arbor, Michigan

Vine Books is an imprint of Servant Publications
especially designed to serve evangelical Christians.

While every effort has been made to trace copyright hold-
ers, if there should be any error or omission, the publishers
will be happy to rectify this at the first opportunity.

Chapters entitled "All-American to All-Martha," "Little
White Note in Copehagen," and "Calico Hospice Lady" are
abbreviated versions of chapters from the book *Remember, I
Love You: Martha's Story*, Charlie Shedd, HarperCollins 1990.
Used by permission.

Published by Servant Publications
P.O. Box 8617
Ann Arbor, Michigan 48107

Cover design by Multnomah Graphics/Printing
Cover illustration by Myles Pinkney
Text design by K. Kelly Bonar
Interior illustration by Paula Murphy

　　　　97 98 10 9

Printed in the United States of America
ISBN 0-89283-854-X

Library of Congress Cataloging–in–Publication Data
Shedd, Charlie W.
　　　Brush of an angel's wing / Charlie W. Shedd
　　　　　p.　　cm.
　　　ISBN 0-89283-854-X : $14.99
　　　1. Angels--Miscellanea.　　I. Title.
　　　BT966.2.S53　1994
235' .3--dc20　　　　　　　　　　　　　　　94-5877
　　　　　　　　　　　　　　　　　　　　　　CIP

Contents

Credo for the Angel Believer

I believe in a loving God
Whose angels are never far away.
Therefore, even when things seem to the contrary,
I believe his universe and my life in it
are unfolding as they should
and everything is on schedule.

Alert to the Happy Surprises

All the time God is waiting
with his holy nudges,
holy whispers,
holy surprises,
holy angels.

The Lady and Her Horse

"*I* need to see you right away!"

It was a plaintive voice on the phone and obviously troubled. So we made an appointment. And that afternoon as she came through my door, everything about her spoke of true class. Attractive, intelligent, a young instructor at the University of Houston, working on her doctorate. But she was bothered, and she'd come to me because she was a regular reader of my column in *The Houston Post*.

"This morning," she began, "the strangest thing happened. It was 2:00 A.M. when I woke with a start. I turned on the lights and looked around. There was this loud noise in my ears like a horse neighing."

She went on to say that she owned two horses which she kept in a pasture five miles from her apartment. She was from west Texas, and she had grown up with horses. She and her horses, she said, were very much in tune.

When the sound died away, she turned off the lights

and settled down once more. But in a few minutes, there came the neighing again. This time she sat up in bed and waited. Then it came for the third time, loud, clear.

Of course, she thought of her own horses, and suddenly she knew: she must go to the pasture! *How silly can I get?* she asked. *Am I losing my mind? It's two o'clock in the morning!*

Still, she knew she must go. So she dressed, called the night man to bring her car, and drove to the stable.

"Please don't say one word until I'm through," she continued. "It all seems so impossible. When I got there, I found my palomino mare standing in broken wire, neighing her lungs out. Some horses are like that, you know. They seem to sense that the wise thing to do is 'don't move and call for help.'"

So, the mare stood still while her mistress untangled the barbed wire. Talking to her, soothing her, she set her free. Then some ointment for the superficial cuts and back home to bed.

"What do you all think happened?" she asked in her lovely Texas drawl. "I couldn't really have heard my horse through the sounds of the night, the hum of the freeway, the noise of a big city like this. And the horses are five miles away! What *do* you think happened?"

I didn't laugh. Instead, we talked. I told her some of my own unusual experiences. And then I told her what I thought happened.

But before I tell you what I told her—
What do *you* think happened?

Every night around the family dinner table we had a fun ritual called *Interesting Things*. Each of us would share one of our day's events. An exciting moment, sometimes a funny one. Maybe a somber happening, something heavy. When it came my turn that night, I told about the neighing horse. Then I asked this collection of interesting characters, "What do you think happened?"

They were quiet for a time. Very unusual for our family of seven. At last Peter broke the silence. (He's now a university professor, but even at twelve, he was already a philosopher.) *"Dad,"* he said, *"either the lady is lying, or God told her to go see about her horse."*

Of course, they asked me what I told her. So I gave it to them exactly as I'd given my answer to her:

I believe that the God who created us did not go off and leave us. In his love he is constantly trying to reach us, lead us, guide us. Or maybe he wants to warn us, detour us, perhaps bring us to an abrupt stop for our own good. I believe that all around us, all the time, his angels are there wanting to direct us. And for what reason? Because he loves us.

So why don't we experience his blessings more often? Is it because we are too busy, too preoccupied, trying to run our lives our way?

Yet all the time he is waiting with his holy nudges, holy whispers, holy surprises, holy angels. Always he wants to bless us, use us, love us with the wonders of his love.

But Where Were
the Angels?

$\mathcal{B}$ut where were the angels in the young lady's story? She hadn't seen any, had she? Did you?

No, She hadn't. Yet that is exactly how angels do things. And when we study the Bible's angels, we see this clearly: angels are not looking for publicity or visibility. Apparently all they have in mind is to get their job done. Sometimes completely behind the scenes, sometimes so near we can almost feel their breath.

On other occasions, they seem to send their blessings from a distance. Across town. Across state lines. Across continents. Across pastures and busy freeways. Sometimes with lightning speed. Sometimes so slowly we think they'll never get here.

Always that's how angels are. They operate their way, not ours. Or rather, they do things for God, *his* way.

All this is why I like the phrase the *brush of an angel's wing.*

Some of the stories you'll be reading are like the lady

and her horse. Nobody even thought about angels until it was over. Then to the thinking mind come all these questions: However could that have happened? Divine intervention? What's going on here? Angels?

Your Most Unusual Happening

"*W*hat was *your* most unusual experience?" Ask it in almost any gathering of friends. If this is one of your relaxed moments together, you're in for a great time.

"I met someone who made all the difference."

"That phone call came at exactly the right moment."

"Oh yes, and the unexpected check arrived just in the nick of time."

"This event meshed with that event as though it had been planned without our knowing. We could hardly believe it."

"I had decided to move there, but instead I came here. Think what I'd have missed if I hadn't come!"

"But doesn't that work both ways? We stayed put instead of going, and then we heard some things later that made us ever so glad we didn't go."

"I will never forget how an unexpected warning saved my life. I'm not even sure what it was. A sudden sound? A sensation? A movement? I guess I'll never really know, but I've often asked myself, was it an angel?"

"It was our first day in the class, and everyone said she was the most boring teacher on campus. Yet she and I hit it off like best friends. And because of her, I'm in an exciting field I'd never even thought of."

"Let me tell you about the little dog that came to our door one night. We didn't want a dog, but we kept her and were we ever glad! The fireman said if it hadn't been for the fuss she raised, we'd never have made it out in time."

"Ruthie, I can't believe I met you when I did. I was about to make a serious mistake. That was thirty years ago. Thank you, Ruthie. Thank you, Lord!"

"And thank you for your smile, Stranger. How did you know I needed a smile right then?"

Bark, bark, little dog. Ring on, you telephones. Bring us those letters, you mailmen. On and on. Big things. Small things. Very small things like one line from a book, one verse from a hymn, the sound of a bird outside our window.

What shall we call it? Chance? Coincidence? Luck? Fate? And if these are not the right labels, what label shall we use? I like *the brush of an angel's wing.*

Seventy-Eight

I am seventy-eight years old and that's a great age. Some people say that's "old," and some days I think they're right. Yet most of the time I love being seventy-eight. You keep on living and you'll see. You'll know more than you've ever known: about yourself, about other people, and about the Lord you've lived with.

For almost sixty years I've had the fun of loving people as their pastor. Now I have the fun of loving as an author.

Because I write, I am invited far and wide for speaking engagements. In seminars, workshops, conferences, churches, schools, military settings, every age and every type. Sometimes I talk on angels. Then we discuss, and from these discussions I hear hundreds of angel stories. Straight from where they've happened I hear them and they make me think—thoughts for today and yesterday.

When you are seventy-eight an interesting thing may happen to your memory. You might not be able to remember today's items like you once could. Here you stand at the foot of your stair asking, "Did I just come down from there or was I going up for something?" When that happens, I hope you'll be able to laugh at yourself. But along with those moments come others when you'll be saying, "See how good the Lord is." At seventy-eight he takes me back down the roads I've traveled. So many things I'd almost forgotten come to meet me. Clear, exact, in minute detail they return to say, "Remember me?"

When that began happening to me, I made this decision: *Before I go to heaven there are some things I'd like to share with my family, my friends, my readers.* Why should those of us with more years in the faith leave here without passing along what we know? And so I decided to write *Brush of An Angel's Wing.*

We hear so much these days about the New Testament church. Yet, I wonder what would happen if all God's children today really *did* believe like the New Testament church believed. They believed they could know the Lord personally. They could walk with him on the road. In dire circumstances he would send his angels. He would loose them from their chains. He'd give them the words they needed as they stood before judges. He would also tell them when to go forward, when to retreat, when to stand still and wait.

Why could they believe this way? They could believe because they believed that with the Holy Spirit, *God would be with them all the time.* Why shouldn't Christians of our modern and scientific age experience the mysteries of God as much as people in Bible times? Didn't Jesus say we should? Don't you think he wants us to have that kind of faith today?

Yet the closer I get to the sunset of life, the more I am sure of this, too. Being a New Testament believer is not a matter of believing only. This kind of life is a way of *awareness*. It is a way of life which capitalizes on the goodness of God. It celebrates the realness of God. And it stands ever more amazed at the way he works in our lives when we let him. Awake or asleep, any time, any day, anywhere, we may feel the brush of an angel's wing.

And when that happens we will know why the Scripture says:

> *"God will order his angels to take good care of you."*
> **Luke 4:10 TEV**

Angels in My Teens

You've had moments you'll never forget, and three of mine happened in my teens. Thirteen, eighteen, and nineteen— three moments of stark drama in one boy's life.

The first saved me from drowning. The second kept me from burning. The third came on my first pastoral visit. It was in a barn, with the farmer who had heard a voice from his haymow. All three for me were high, holy happenings. And they gave me a reverence for life which has never gone away.

A Hand
in the Water Pipe

The Cedar River runs through my hometown. Wide, deep, winding, this has to be one of America's most beautiful rivers. And I should know. I grew up on it.

As the Cedar passes by downtown, there is a churning section of water called *The Millrace*. Standing on the river bank it's plain to see why they labeled this a race. Fallen limbs from the upstream trees, worn out and broken boats, old tires, and trash of many kinds battled each other in the millrace.

More than sixty years ago, when I was a boy, one landmark at the millrace was a giant pipe. Purpose of the pipe? To keep the millrace from rushing its debris downstream. Manufacturing plants, factories, and businesses had been built along the river's edge. Their foundations of concrete, brick, and wood were important both to owners and employee paychecks. For this reason a giant screen had been attached to the pipe's outlet. Here, the debris could be halted to protect the downstream walls and underpinnings. Every few months the screen would be removed, cleaned, and the rubbish hauled harmlessly away.

Almost every boy who grew up along the Cedar River became a good swimmer. Swimming was our thing. Showing off was our thing, too, and all those signs along the millrace bank were a magnet drawing us on. *Danger, Strong Current, Undertow, Swimming Strictly Forbidden.* But you know how boys are. For us the taunting question was, "How close can *you* get to the big pipe?" This day I decided it was my turn. I would show them something, and I did.

It was full-river season, with extra danger because the water was high. What I didn't know was that water would also be high in the pipe. At the top there would be no more than a few inches of air. Six? Ten?

Sometimes there is a fine line between good sense and plain foolishness. And this day I crossed the line.

Into the water I went and started toward the pipe; one eye on the current and the other on my friends. But the current was powerful enough to pull even an accomplished swimmer into the tunnel. Before I knew what had happened, I was swept into the pipe, sucked under the water by the powerful rush of the millrace! Truth: I was about to drown.

If you were about to drown, you would have an amazing experience. Like a fast-forward video, everything you ever did would go racing through your mind. The good, the beautiful, the bad, your hopes and dreams —all speeding by. Awesome. Unbelievable.

At thirteen, boys don't think of dying. But I did then.

Boys don't pray much either, but I did that too.

Then suddenly I felt a lift, as though a hand were taking me up to the air.

I filled my lungs and fought against the undertow. But still I was little competition for the downward pull. Down to the bottom again. All this time I was struggling—struggling against the current, struggling to get back where I came in. There would be no escape at the other end. The heavy screen was much too stubborn to let a boy through.

Then came that hand again. Something, *someone* lifted me up for air again. Three or four times it happened. And each time, when the hand was gone, it was back to the bottom for me, no match for the pull.

Still, I kept struggling, turning around, heading back toward the entrance. Yet with each turn now I seemed to hear a voice saying, "Forget the screen! Head for the outward exit!" Then once more I felt the hand, this time turning me hard, hurling me toward the screen end. With one mighty shove, up, up, and out of the tunnel, up to unlimited air.

"See the wooden fence, Charlie? Go for it. Hold on. Hold on till the lifeguards come. See them coming fast to the rescue?"

I do not remen ber all that happened then, but this one thing I will never forget. As they pulled me into their boat, the captain said, "Were you ever lucky, kid. Yesterday we took the screen off to clean the thing. Real lucky."

Why did the lifeguards take the screen off yesterday? Pure routine? Or did it happen yesterday to save the life of a teenage showoff today?

Then came the barrage of lifeguard questions: "What's your name? Where do you live? Why were you swimming so close? What was it like in there? How do you feel?"

Then the captain asked one final question: *"Weren't there two of you in there? Somehow we got the idea there were two."*

How many times through the years have I asked myself, "Why didn't I answer, 'There really were two. But the other one had to leave early to answer another call.'"

Some years ago, we were visiting with a group of friends —a real heady bunch, the kind where any subject might be introduced. That night the topic was extraordinary happenings. When it was my turn, I told about that hand in the water pipe.

One of those friends was a non-believer. A brainy man, a thinker, professor at the university. He listened intently as any thinker would. Then he moved in with his explanation. "Don't you understand, Charlie, you were young and strong. Often in emergencies there is a rush of strength from deep in the subconscious. That's your explanation. Besides, what if there is a God who runs the universe? With all he has to do, you don't think he'd have time for one fool boy in one tunnel on one river, do you?"

To which a responsive young lady in the group replied, *"Oh, but didn't you know? God has angels, too?"*

And for sixty-five years, ever since I felt that hand in the tunnel, I've believed she had the answer. *HE DOES!*

"In my distress... I cried to my God
for help.... He reached down from on high and
took hold of me; he drew me out
of deep waters."
Psalm 18:6, 16 NIV

Miracle in the Oil Vat

$\mathcal{T}$he dry rendering works of a packing plant "send forth a stinking savor." (That's the biblical term for repugnant smell.) These odors originate from the butchers' left-overs. Entrails cooking at high temperature and uglies boiling in oil produce a product called "cracklings" and "chitterlings." For what purpose? Feed for animals and dollars for the packer. Big money from the waste and leftovers.

I went to college on a football scholarship. Most "scholarships" sixty years ago meant tuition and fees, plus a guaranteed job for room and board. But they also carried another benefit. Summers, the athletic department would do its best to find us work. Preferably hard work to keep us in condition for the gridiron.

The summer before my junior year, one of the packing plant executives had a heart for football. There were two openings in dry rendering. Lucky me. Lucky my buddy. Lucky as in higher wages than other jobs for athletes. But very unlucky in another sense.

All summer we were socially ostracized. No amount

of scrubbing could remove the smell from our hair, skin, and clothes. Because of the odor that seemed to follow us around, we were unwelcome almost anywhere. So my buddy and I roomed together, ate together, and socialized together—not that it was much of a social life.

I do not remember all the details of the cooking process with absolute recall. Anyone who ever worked in dry rendering would make a concerted effort to forget it. But I do remember this much—all the leftovers from the butchering process were dumped into deep vats—vats two or three times as deep as the tallest man. Large spigots above the vats released hot oil into the mixture, and the cooking process began.

In addition to hauling wheelbarrows full of cracklings and chitterlings to the cooker, on occasion we were to clean our own vat. One day I was at the bottom of my vat, ready to begin scrubbing. In my busyness and my preoccupation with the smell I did not notice that after · went down, someone borrowed my ladder. This pro cedure, as you can imagine also, was very much against the company rules. But some new worker hadn't learned the rules. (As you can imagine, the drop-out rate in dry rendering was astronomical.)

Fascinating, how one mistake sometimes follows another. Mistake number two, which was very, *very* much against company regulations: someone turned the wrong valve, and the hot oil poured into the vat. Into *my* vat, pouring down on *me*!

I kept my head down and raced toward the only possible outlet. It was a very small pipe for letting in water, much too flimsy for any man at any weight. And certainly much too weak for the weight of a college football player.

Did I pray? I most certainly did, and the answer came clear. "UP THE PIPE. THERE IS NO OTHER WAY!" So up I went, fast, hand over hand on the bending pipe, greasy with oil, too hot for a man's hands. Yet up I went and out.

Impossible, and everyone at the plant knew how impossible. "He couldn't a done it. Ain't nobody gonna do that. You wanna bet?" (In dry rendering they get their jollies where they can.) So they made up a pool, and one by one they tried it. Wiping the pipe dry, making sure it was cool, they gave it all they had. So did I, but like the old veteran said, "Ain't nobody gonna do that." And nobody did! Including me. Even with dried hands and cool vat, never again.

I muse on all those explanations such as "buried potential," "latent strength," "surges of dormant power." But thinking back on the oil vat escape and that hand in the water pipe, I think they fit right in with what I call "the brush of an angel's wing."

Grandma Minnie's Fried Chicken

Sugar Creek Church is a dear little gathering of Iowa farmers. White clapboard church building to match the white houses all around. Big red barns. Tall silos. Great spreading fields of corn and soybeans. Haystacks, cows in the pasture, sheep, pigs, horses, and ponies. And when I was their hungry young pastor, I saw chickens here, chickens there, chickens, chickens everywhere.

"Preacher Boy," they would say, "when you drive down our lane, the roosters run and lay their heads on the chopping block." Preacher Boy was their name for me, and why not? I was no minister, only a college student. A lover of farm folks, and of chicken.

I agreed to go to Sugar Creek because my Bible professor said, "You've been thinking about the ministry. Now here's your chance to see what it's like. I've been to Sugar Creek, and I can guarantee you won't be sorry."

So, late Saturday, tired from playing football; tired from celebrating another win (This was the year we had a good team); off I went, much too tired to think up a sermon along the way.

I knew most of these excuses ahead of time. They were my excuses to my Bible professor. "Oh, just go on down there," he'd say, "pick some Bible story you like. Tell them what it means to you. Smile. Give them some of your jokes. You'll love it. Go!"

So I went, and it was everything my Bible professor said it would be. Anyone lucky enough to be the student pastor at Sugar Creek would thank the Lord forever. And I have.

On my very first Sunday, I had chicken at Grandma Minnie's. She was little. She was old. She had pure white hair. And she was just plain *glad* like few people I've ever met. Gladness in her eyes, gladness in her voice, gladness in her soul. And could she ever make fried chicken. For this I was very, very glad.

For years Grandma Minnie had been teaching the Adult Bible Class. Straight from the Good Book and straight from her loving heart she taught. Looking back later, I realized she had literally kept Sugar Creek Church together during some of those years—especially in years when the pastoral leadership was somewhat lacking.

That first Sunday we became fast friends. Her husband Howard was a pleasant man, quiet. He loved to putter about the farmyard. So after eating his fill, he'd excuse himself, and I'd have another round of chicken… plus theology… plus advice.

"Preacher Boy," Aunt Minnie would begin, "we just plain love you. You stand up there and smile. You tell us a Bible story. It's usually one we've already heard so we know when you get mixed up. Then somebody shakes their head and you laugh. So we laugh and that's all right. But do you know mostly why we love you? It's because for so long we've been listening to how bad we are, been hearing about hellfire and sin. Well, we know about sin. We know that first-hand. But we like to think we might be a little bit all right. So here you come telling us God made us beautiful and he never gives up on us. Then you tell us he sent Jesus to clean up what needs cleaning up so we can be beautiful again.

"Now you listen to me, Preacher Boy. Don't you ever get away from that, because that's the gospel. That's the good news, and nobody ever got enough of it. So have another piece of chicken and listen to this too. Someday you'll be preaching in a big church somewhere, and I won't be there. But I'll be listening and smiling and cheering you on. And if you ever get even a little bit off the good news you'll feel a zap and that will be me, Minnie, zapping you from heaven."

Then she would say, "There's so little chicken left, why don't you just clean it up?" And I would.

So where do the angels fit into this story? Once again I did not *see* any angels with my eyes. Yet I certainly felt Someone looking out for me. If you had seen my junky, old convertible, and the junky motorcycle that some-times took its place, you'd know what I mean. It was fifty miles from my college to the little church. Some of those roads were dirt roads—mud when it rained. Some of the weekends were snowy, cold, icy. With that kind of travel and my ancient machinery, I returned again and again to my favorite "angel" promise from the Book—

> *He shall give his angels charge over thee*
> *to keep thee in all thy ways.*
> **Psalm 91:11 KJV**

Voice from the Haymow

*H*ave you ever heard a voice you couldn't locate? Behind you, before you, off there to the side or up above you? You know you heard that voice, but from where did it come? Who was it? Nobody in sight, no one near. Are my ears playing tricks? Am I losing my mind? Where can I go to talk this over? Would they laugh at me?

Lee thought they would laugh. Lee was a member of the Sugar Creek Church. On my third Sunday at Sugar Creek, Lee waited until everyone had gone, then he made his way to my little Ford. I could tell he was nervous and hesitant. I learned later that he'd had very little experience with the clergy and he was wondering what the new Preacher Boy would think. But Lee had decided to risk it, so almost in a whisper he began.

"Preacher Boy, I've got a problem. I've got to talk with someone real bad. Could you come to my place this afternoon? Don't go in the house. Meet me at the barn.

I'll be waiting for you by the haymow steps."

So there I was at the haymow steps for my first pastoral call. The first ever.

After working through his initial hesitations, Lee came straight to the point. "Sometime last year I was standing here by these steps when I heard a voice up in the haymow. Clear and plain the voice said, 'Lee, God wants you to build a calf feeder. This will be the best calf feeder ever, and here's how I want you to build it.' Then the voice gave me exact measurements. How high, how wide, how long, and how every piece should fit. Let's go out to the feed lot. I'll show you."

Even I, who knew exactly nothing about calves and their feeding, was instantly impressed. A true work of art. Deep green blending with bright yellow, and a calf at every opening. The genius of this calf feeder was that each calf would be temporarily enclosed in its own space. Bully calves had no way of taking feed away from the timid. Yet that wasn't the only positive factor in Lee's calf feeder. By some dependable method, when each calf had eaten its ration, the feeder shut down. Then another calf would take its place in that stanchion.

"There it is," Lee said, "exactly like it was told to me. Same measurements, same design, straight from the voice in the haymow. Whose voice was it? An angel? I've wondered about it a million times. Whoever it was, he told me several times he was speaking for God. What do *you* think?"

"What I think," said the Preacher Boy, "is that it's beginning to rain. Let's go back in the barn and talk this over."

When we sat down on the hay bales, I thanked him for sharing his wonderful story. Then I told him I believed every word he said because from age thirteen I'd known there were angels. And we both agreed—it isn't everyone you can talk to about angels.

For a long time we sat with our thoughts and questions. Exactly how do angels work? Why don't they come more often? Why do they come when they do?

Then Lee told me about other things he'd made. That lever which turned off the windmill when the water was high enough; the barn door latch, absolutely impossible for even the trickiest horse to undo; a chicken waterer, so effective everyone who saw it wanted one. And each of his inventions, he said, seemed to come from outside himself. Sometimes in a dream, then a sudden inspiration. Or maybe it wasn't outside himself at all. Others came with time, like a slow shaping from way down inside.

Mostly I listened, but I also told him other times when I thought angels had been at work in my life. I shared about my rescue from the oil vat and many small experiences I called the *brush of an angel's wing*. He liked that phrase and we used it often in the fast friendship born that day at the haymow steps.

Now it was growing dark and nearly time for supper. "Let's go to the house, Preacher Boy. Nobody makes chicken like Leora. And I bet you'll agree you never put your mouth to anything as good as Leora's pecan pie."

Just before we left the barn I remembered what I'd read somewhere: preachers ought to pray on special occasions. So Lee and I knelt there in the hay and thanked the Lord for sending his angels our way. I thanked him again for my rescue experiences, and I thanked him for Lee's inventive mind. Then the prayer ended with this simple request: "Lord, may we both be ever more alert for even the smallest brush of an angel's wing."

As we headed for the house, Lee asked another question: "Preacher Boy, do you think it might have been an angel brought you and me together?"

I told him I felt absolutely sure it was an angel.

I also told him this as we ate together... and he was absolutely right about Leora's chicken and her pecan pie.

Last summer I made a trip back to Sugar Creek. Some of the memories had faded over sixty years. Others had been preserved clear and forever in the memory album of my mind.

Grandma Minnie's long lane is still there, and so is her house. I could almost see her smiling out the kitchen window, holding a plate of fried chicken.

I asked if anyone remembered Lee's calf feeder. "Sure do," they replied. "Fact is, he patented it."

I spoke with Lee's son, an Episcopal priest and hospital chaplain. He'd never heard the haymow story. "But it sounds just like my dad," he responded. "All his life he was big on angels and extraordinary happenings. I could tell you some other things I guess nobody would believe, except maybe you and me."

Before I left Sugar Creek, I drove out by Lee's big barn. The calf feeder was gone, but the memory was still there clear, vivid. As I stood in the barnyard, I could feel it all again. One nervous young farmer telling the Preacher Boy his far-out story. And I could almost see the two of us kneeling there in the hay. Two amazed believers quietly praising the Lord for his goodness... and especially for his angels.

Where Have All the Angels Gone?

Talk about angels in almost any group, and you may experience what this questioner felt:

> Why do people raise their eyebrows when we talk about angels? Even in Sunday School, you bring up angels and people look at you like you came from some funny farm. Wherever did this idea originate that believing in angels is a bit too much for normal Christians?

Unfortunate, but true. Ours is a nation of closet believers in angels. These are the host of people hoping that sometime, somewhere, they will meet somebody who will listen and understand. Someone who will say, "Welcome aboard. I'm an angel believer, too."

"I'll Buy You
an Ice-Cream Soda"

S o many times I've thanked the Lord that Dr. B. was my college Bible professor. He was the one who persuaded me to try Sugar Creek. But long prior to that we'd become fast friends.

Our friendship began with his first assignment. We were to write a paper called "My Number One Religious Experience." Nothing major. One or two pages, and keep it simple.

I wrote on my rescue from the water pipe at age thirteen. He loved it. The very next day he said, "Let's go out after class. I'll buy you an ice-cream soda." That was an invitation I heard often. Is it any wonder Dr. B. became my all-time favorite teachers?

Between Dr. B. and me all roads were open. We could talk about anything. My unexplainable happenings and his. His extraordinary moments and mine.

Why was I on a football scholarship at this particular school? Even the universities were looking for big tackles.

So why was I here at this modest denominational college? Looking back, I think I know the real reason. Right then I needed a friend like Dr. B., and I thanked the Lord for my good fortune. My first year in seminary Greek, I realized too that Dr. B. and his angels had been getting me ready for something altogether different.

Chicago

*C*hicago is only three hundred miles from my college
town, and less than that from Sugar Creek. But for
me it might as well have been three million. I had never
seen so many people together in one place. As I was
growing up, money for travel was absolutely nil. For
everyone else I knew, same song, next verse. So here
was the country boy among those swirling masses, and
I felt lost.

Our seminary was located in one of Chicago's rough-
est neighborhoods. Shortly after I arrived, the FBI's most
wanted criminal was shot as he came out of a theater
across our street. Up the street, another major tourist
attraction. This, the site of a famous gangland murder
fresh from its happening the year before.

Some of us in the freshman class needing financial
support were given jobs for board and room. Lucky me.
I latched onto the prime position of assistant to the
night watchman.

Every night I set my clock for midnight and made the
campus rounds with a flashlight. Our school lawns

were the only green grass for miles around, so we had many visitors: late night drunks on picnics, couples getting acquainted, homeless looking for a soft place to sleep. So, after clearing the grounds of the uninvited guests, it was back to bed in my own private room.

Mine was the only private room on campus, but the accommodations were not as plush as they sound. My "private" room was one huge room in the Commons, a massive Gothic building. By day the Great Room was everyone's favorite. Here we ate our meals and attended special events. Laugh, men, laugh. This was the one place on campus we could have fun. But at night this large, happy room became my cavernous bedroom. Spooky.

The seminary bookstore was located in the Commons, adjacent to the Great Room. Too many times the store had been robbed, so someone needed to be sure it didn't happen again. Night after night found me in the Great Room, sleeping my shallow sleep, gun under pillow, ever alert.

All this was a major part of my introduction to Chicago. "Never fear, Charlie is here!" was my classmates' familiar quip. The bookstore people also said it often, smiling. Only the night watchman didn't say it. He knew the possibilities.

Because you will be curious, I never once used my gun. There was action now and then—enough action to teach me some secrets about projecting the voice. In a cavernous room like the Common's Great Room, if you practice you can make your voice sound like many voices. Those who dared to enter did not tarry.

Looking back from here, I wonder how I did it. Country boy in the big city, scared silly. Yet for one whole year I slept in the Great Room, and I did it for two good reasons. Reason one: the job paid a bit more than room and board. Reason two: I believed in angels.

Over and over again that year I repeated this favorite promise of The Book:

> *He shall give his angels charge over thee,*
> *to keep thee in all thy ways.*
> **Psalm 91:11 KJV**

"Write on Anything You Want —Except Angels"

 or second semester freshman Greek, we were assigned a fifty-page thesis on any subject of our choice. All we needed for a base was to verify our writing from the New Testament. That would be easy for me.

Can you imagine what a nice surprise it was when my Greek professor also invited me to stay after class? Only nice surprise it wasn't. No ice-cream soda. No friendly chat either. As nearly as I remember, his words of advice went something like this: "I'm sorry, we cannot let you write on angels. I have taken it up with my superior and he agrees. 'Angelology,' as we call it, raises far more questions than it answers. It disturbs more than it blesses. Of course you realize I am telling you this for your own good. As members of the seminary faculty, we keep before us the fact that we are preparing young men for the ministry. Therefore, thinking of your future, we must warn you against these controversial themes. I feel sure you will understand."

I didn't. I also told him I didn't, which was mistake number one. Mistake two was when I asked a personal question: What did he and his superior do with the Christmas angels, the ones I had written about for my college professor? To which came this chilly answer: "We must remember that much of the Bible is history, and we should respect it as such."

That, I guess, is what he did with all those biblical angels. He respected them as history. To put it mildly, the more I argued, the more he "lost his erudite." To put it mildly, too, I was lucky to get through Greek.

Yet the whole fiasco was not all disaster. Out of that experience I did some pensive pondering and came to these conclusions which never left me:

a. The Bible *is* history, but not first. *First, the Bible is our heavenly Father's guide to victorious living today.*

b. When someone tells me an angel story, or when I experience the brush of an angel's wing myself, I test it by these two questions:

1. Does it have verification in biblical accounts of the angels?

2. Historically, and especially in my own history, was the outcome helpful to at least one person, or even to many?

When I think back to that first year in seminary, my early thoughts focus on those scary nights in the Great Room of our Commons. Then I remember my professor's thoughts on the Bible and how we should look at it. So I smile and ask myself, "If my professor had been trying to sleep where I was trying to sleep, gun under pillow, I wonder if he might have preferred angels *as the real thing* rather than history?"

I also wonder, if he were teaching today, with the plethora of fresh interest in the angel themes, would he alter his position?

Billy Graham gave us a start with his wonderful book on angels. *Guideposts* magazine cleared away more of the negative attitude with their classics on "His Mysterious Ways." Even our secular best-seller lists reveal the fresh interest.

So turn on the TV, angel lovers. Dial the radio, open a magazine, scan your newspaper. Angels have finally come forward big-time, prime time. Supernatural things, extraordinary happenings, events unexplainable, all seem to be taking center stage. Meaning what? Meaning: behind the scenes there is a latent hunger to believe angels are as up-to-date as our next heartbeat.

What Is an Angel?

*Praise ye the Lord from the heavens:
praise him in the heights.
Praise ye him, all his angels.*

Psalm 148:1–2

What Is an Angel?

J have shared with you some of my own encounters with angels, as well as other people's experiences. But if you are like others I've met at workshops and seminars, you may still be asking, "But exactly what is an angel?"

Angels have amazed and puzzled us for centuries. We cannot comprehend the mind of God, nor do we understand the ways of his angels. We do not know why God sends his angels at one time and not at another. At times we have been surprised by the brush of an angel's wing. In other situations we have prayed for an angel but no response. These are mysteries which we may never solve in our present existence.

But if we look at the Bible; at the way angels interacted with humans; at what we do know about God; we can make some conclusions about what angels are and what they do. I have frequently been asked if angels are merely another form of God or an extension of God. I believe the Bible makes this clear—they are not. So, here's that question again: what *is* an angel?

The two words which come closest to a true biblical answer are "manifestation" and "servant." Most of us know what a servant is, but what is a manifestation? Putting together several dictionary meanings we arrive at this definition: To manifest means to reveal, prove, display, and put beyond doubt the nature of that which is being manifested.

Since God is love and angels exist to manifest and serve him, then what angels do is to reveal, prove, and display God's love.

Angels carry the love of God where he wants it this day, this moment. And since the Heavenly Father's love is limitless, another fact follows—angels may be found doing anything, any time, any place, any way to help God's people.

For an authentic record of angel activities, we can do no better than to turn to the Bible. Here, straight from Scripture, we see the vast panorama of angel activity.

- Angels announce (carry messages)—Luke 1:26-33, Luke 2:8-12
- Angels warn—Matthew 2:13
- Angels advise—Matthew 1:18-23
- Angels praise God—Luke 2:13-14
- Angels eat—Psalm 78:25
- Angels fly—How many times do you think angels fly in the Bible? Many. Find twelve.
- Angels ascend and descend—Genesis 28:12, John 1:51
- Angels guard—Psalm 34:7

- Angels protest—Zechariah 3:4
- Angels comfort—Acts 27:23-24
- Angels heal—Job 33:20-24
- Angels speak the truth—Hebrews 2:2
- Angels communicate (Angels not only talk *to* people; they talk *with* them.)—Zechariah 1:9, Luke 1:34-35
- Angels preach—Galatians 1:8
- Angels proclaim—Revelation 5:2
- Angels find the lost—Genesis 16:7
- Angels feed and provide—1 Kings 19:5-7
- Angels minister to Christ—Matthew 4:11, Mark 1:13
- Angels minister to people—Hebrews 1:14
- Angels set free—Acts 5:19, Acts 12:7-9
- Angels give direction—Acts 8:26
- Angels save from death—Daniel 6:22
- Angels fight our battles—Exodus 33:2
- Angels stir up the waters—John 5:4
- Angels worship—Isaiah 6:2-3, Revelation 5:11-12

This is a list of twenty-five things angels did in Bible times. And the list could go to nearly three hundred additional acts and actions. It's a startling figure, isn't it? Nearly three hundred times we see angels doing something for the Lord.

Suppose now we were to add that list to another list. If we could hear from everyone since Bible times—everyone in history who ever had one experience they might call *the brush of an angel's wing*—wouldn't that be an awesome witness to God's eternal love for his own?

❦ F I V E ❧

God's Traffic Ways

*"You came into my life right then
and I felt the brush of an angel's wing."*

It may have been a friend, perhaps a stranger, a member of the family. They were blessed and you were a part of the blessing.

So does that make you an angel? Sorry, the biblical answer has to be "No." From both Old Testament and

New comes the clear answer. We've seen it once. Let's look at it again.

"What is man that thou art mindful of him?...
Thou hast made him a little lower than the angels."
Psalm 8:4–5 and Hebrews 2:7

"Then won't we be angels in heaven?" Again the biblical answer is a definite "No."

Yet here on earth and as long as we live,
this is our calling:
All who aim to become real followers of our Lord
will try to live so much in tune with him
that any time he needs us
we are ready to become
traffic ways for his angels.

Fire and
the Football Player

In our university town, a big and powerful all-American football player was jogging early one morning. It was still dark and, from the hill where he ran, he saw a fire by the side of the road. Speeding up his pace, he ran as fast as he could; and because he could run all-American fast, he saved a woman's life.

She had been in a single car accident with no one anywhere near. She didn't know how it happened. She was on her way to work, very early, and she must have fallen asleep. But one thing she did know: when she hit the telephone pole, her car burst into flames. The crash also crushed the front end, fender, floorboard, and bent the driver's door. The woman was trapped inside, one leg pinned to the floor.

You should know, before I tell you the rest of the story, that this particular football player is a devout believer. From childhood, his mother taught him many things about the Lord. She taught him that God has a plentiful supply of all the strength anyone could ever need—a strength available to him if he stayed in tune with the Divine.

Arriving at the fiery scene, he knew this woman needed his help badly. So, with his mighty arms, he ripped the broken door from the woman's car, freed her leg, and saved her life.

By now others had come, including the police. Seeing that everything was in good hands, the all-American football player continued his jogging.

When the woman told the police what had happened they asked, "Who was he?"

"I have no idea," she answered. *"I wonder if he was an angel."*

But the story doesn't end there. Someone at the scene knew the football player's customary morning route, and they tracked him down.

"Were you at the scene?" the police and reporters asked. "Sure," he admitted. "Then why didn't you stay to tell us what happened. Give us your name?"

"Why should I?" he asked. "You were there. I needed to finish my run and hurry to class."

When they interviewed him on television, he was his usual self. Again he quoted his mother to the effect that God provides strength for life's emergencies. Pure humility. Do what the Lord needs doing. Thank your mother and move along.

For a touch of whimsy to finish the story, one of the coaches, the staff clown, quipped, "What our team needs is more mamma's boys."

Call from
Grandma Wehking

There are some special freedoms in a church which numbers by the thousands. One is that the pastor can have his favorites and nobody notices.

Grandma Wehking was one of my favorites. We shared everything. She told me her troubles, and I told her mine. She was eighty-three, and her heart was wearing out. The doctors said she might go on living for some time in this condition. On the other hand, they could operate. It would be risky, but if successful, she might have more time to enjoy her family. She had an only son, a daughter-in-law she loved, and three wonderful grandchildren. So what should she do?

I knew about the big decision she was facing. But this one fact had escaped me: the time for her to decide had come. If you were facing such a decision, what would you do? You had to choose whether to operate or take a chance on living longer without surgery? Could you even sleep nights? A soul on the yo-yo: up, down, up, down, yes, no, yes, no?

I was driving along Katy Road, one of the main arteries in and out of Houston. The day was coming to a close, and I was heading back to my office at the church. I would have a mountain of phone calls to return, drop-in visitors to talk with, staff problems to resolve, plus countless other duties of the pastorate. In addition to all this clutter, I needed to go over the agenda for tonight's meeting, and I was running late. Emergencies at the hospital had made it a long afternoon.

Suddenly, as I hurried on, I thought of Grandma Wehking. Only a few minutes before, I had passed the street where I always turned to visit her. By the time she arrived in my thoughts, however, I was three or four miles down the road. But before I could dismiss her from my mind and move to other things, here came an inner urging. Should I turn around and go back, drop by for a moment's visit? NO. I didn't have time, or did I? Maybe I really should. She'd be needing a prayer.

Wavering between "No I can't" and "Yes I should," I finally opted for "Yes I should." Turning my car around, I drove to the little white house and rang her doorbell. Taking longer than usual, she finally arrived and stretched out her arms. "Oh, Charlie," she said, "I'm so glad Jean got in touch with you. I *had* to see you today."

"Tomorrow I must tell the doctor what I've decided. I wanted so much to talk it over once more and pray together. You tell Jean I'm grateful she tracked you down."

Several times again in our short visit she repeated, "I'm

so grateful Jean got through to you. I was afraid she might not find you." So finally, when my curiosity got the best of me, I asked, "Grandma, what is all this about you calling Jean to track me down? I haven't talked with her since early morning."

"Oh," she said, "You haven't talked with Jean? She told me you were at the hospitals and all afternoon I've been praying she would find you. Matter of fact, Charlie, the reason it took me so long to answer the door right now is that I was back in my bedroom praying."

You can believe we "oohed" and "ahhed" about this extraordinary happening. Those were especially wonderful moments we shared together that day. Then I prayed and headed back to my office.

Say it again. Some label these occasions "coincidence," "chance," "destiny." So? So, I call them "the brush of an angel's wing." But by any label we put on them, doesn't the Bible say, "God rules and overrules in the hearts of men?"

And in the hearts of women, too, like Grandma Wehking.

The Fingers on My Car Keys

We can experience angels in so many different ways. Some tell me they feel "an inner glow," a radiance round about them. Others hear music and all their senses say, "Such notes, such harmony could only come from out of this world." Then there are those who report their angels arrive with a lovely fragrance.

For others, light is the signal. Light moving toward them, light beside them, light off there in the distance.

My friend Homer says he senses an angel near when he discovers himself laughing with a certain laugh. "Sometimes," he says, "I laugh so long I almost miss the message."

Others witness that the angels come to them with not one single indicator. Suddenly from out of nowhere they feel the brush of an angel's wing. And who among the angel believers hasn't had this experience? *After* the rescue, the miracle, the blessing—only then did we realize, "That was an angel."

For me, angels have often made themselves known by the touch of a hand. A lift, a pressure, a movement, a warning, a beckoning. But that shouldn't surprise me, should it? Way back there at age thirteen I had my first experience with the hand of an angel.

The Bible often uses "The hand of God" to reveal God's presence. And because of what I've been through, one of my favorite verses will forever be: "I heard the noise of the wings.... The hand of the Lord was strong upon me" (Ezekiel 3:13–14).

But one evening I felt more than God's hand. This time I felt the touch of God through my fingers.

. It was supper time and I drove into my garage with high anticipation. Always high anticipation for any meal with my favorite cook. Yet this time something else came first.

As I turned off the ignition, my fingers simply wouldn't let go.

"What's going on here?" I asked out loud. From somewhere in my heart came the answer.

Go see Roy. Plain. Clear. No question. From that place in my soul where God and I hold dialogue, I knew he was giving an order.

"But it's supper time," I argued. I tend to argue with the Lord when I'm hungry.

"Supper can wait, Charlie. Go."

"But why? Roy was in church yesterday. He looked fine."

The only response was silence. So, before another word, I turned on the ignition and went.

Roy was one of our senior citizens. A nice old man, aging too fast but still able to get around. Roy owned several farms, and every day he'd pay a visit to the country. He'd putter about, stand by the fence and admire the calves, the colts, the lambs. He loved his farms.

Roy lived less than a mile north in a big old house, a real landmark. *Hurry, Charlie. This could be an emergency.*

And it was.

Dashing up the steps, I found the front door locked. From inside came a moan, but because the curtains were drawn I couldn't see. Hearing the moan again and knowing the quickest route, I rushed to the back door.

The door was unlocked. I rushed to the living room and found Roy on the floor, bleeding, calling for help. Knowing that action was more important than explanation, I checked his cuts, and washed the blood away. Then when I had him clean and quiet, I helped him to the couch.

What happened, he said, was that he'd tripped over a stump behind the corn crib and broke his glasses in the fall.

"But how did you ever drive home, Roy? Six miles, seven? With your face cut and no glasses, however did you do it?

"I don't know, Charlie. I guess the Lord was with me."

Sometime within the hour, his wife arrived, and she took over. So after hearing his report, the three of us joined hands and had a prayer.

As I turned to go, he said, "Thank you, Charlie. How did you know I needed you?"

I thought I should wait until later to tell him about those stubborn fingers on my car keys. So I answered, "I think it was an angel, Roy."

"Makes sense," he replied. "I was lying there on the floor, praying you would come."

A verse for Roy. And isn't it for every one of us?

"I sought the Lord and he heard me."
Psalm 34:4

"Go. Right Now."

*I*t was supper time again, and you know what that meant. I was hungry. But this time I was also lonesome, and that *was* unusual. Martha had gone to an inter-denominational women's meeting three towns up the road. She was due home shortly, and we'd be heading for Cecil's Grill—best country cooking for miles around.

From my study I could see both entrances to our big, old house. I kept an eye on the doorways, ready to run and greet her when she arrived. She liked that, and I did, too.

Suddenly, as I sat there wrapping up my day, I had this strange sensation, a sense of doom. Something was wrong somewhere, and I didn't like it. But since the feeling was without location, I turned it off and went back to my busyness.

Then I felt the dark cloud in my heart once more. This time a voice in my head said, *The Haroldsens. They need you.* Beautiful young couple, David and Rebecca. They had moved to our town three months back. Regular attenders at our worship. I had visited in their home, and they were the "I want to know you better" kind. David was a lineman for Rural Electric, and there were three little Haroldsens.

But right then I wanted to be with Martha, so as usual when I'm turning off an Inner Directive, I explained. "She's been gone all day. She'll be home anytime now. We're going to Cecil's." Do you carry on these silent conversations sometimes? Or aloud if nobody's listening? But whether spoken or only thought, who are we reporting to? To ourselves, our conscience? Or is it the Lord?

Whoever or whatever, once more I turned the signal off. I went back to watching for Martha. It really was thirty minutes before she was due home. I tinkered in my office, looking for some way to pass the time until she arrived. Then once again the impulse came, this time with force: *Go! Go now! At once!*

Three times, and that's enough. Three times is my rule. I had learned that I could out-argue the Inner Voice once, sometimes twice, but never three times. My limit was up; so I locked the study door, got in my car, and took off. Only a few blocks and I was there.

As I made my way up the walk, I heard a woman screaming. Could it be Rebecca? In trouble? Dashing up the steps, I opened the door and there she stood: phone in hand, baby in arms, two others hanging to her apron. I will never forget that picture. Utter horror. Panic. Dismay. *They were calling from the office to tell her David had been electrocuted!*

The next sound you hear is that of a breaking heart.

Mine. Or should I say five breaking hearts?

Never in all my life have I felt so sorry for anyone. One lovely lady in one afternoon, a sudden widow. Three little children in one awful moment, fatherless.

What can a minister say in an hour like this? Not much, not right then. All he can do is be there, to touch a hand, to sooth a shattered soul.

Cutting now across the hours of tragedy, I can tell you I was proud of the women from my church. Proud of the Rural Electric folks, too. The men came alone or with their wives to do what they could. Neighbors came, and that was good. The Haroldsens were new people, strangers really, but who in a small town is a stranger when someone's hurting? Food of every kind, flowers of every kind, love—real love, God's pure love.

Then the relatives came and they were one superior collection of young, middle age, old, very old, all quality. The church was packed for David's service. The people in our town were like that. They lived by the introspective credo, "Ask not for whom the bell tolls. It tolls for thee."

Before she went back to live near her parents, Rebecca and I became good friends. Pastor and brokenhearted mother, sharing the pain, discussing it all, wondering. "Why? How could You let this happen, Lord? It simply isn't fair!" We discussed all kinds of things like that, and as the wisdom writer says, "Ever we came out the same door we went in."

Those are awful moments when you feel so helpless. You search for something to say, something to do and you know it's a solemn fact: the one thing needful you can't do. "Come back, David. We need you here." But since you're only talking into empty wishes, you go on talking, go on wondering, sharing the silence, then talking on, wondering on.

One day, three years later, I received a letter from Rebecca. She was marrying again, a very nice man who loved her children. Would I pray for her and for him and all of them together?

I did. So did the people in our church, and I'm sure her family was praying too.

I wish I could tell you Rebecca and her new husband lived happily ever after, but they didn't. Three children were too much for him, and she was alone again. So we came back to the same old questions: "Why? How could You let this happen, Lord? It simply isn't fair."

Today Rebecca is doing quite well, considering. She was extra fine quality, remember? She still hangs tight to that verse from Romans: "All things work together for good to them that love God" (Romans 8:28). She's active in her church, has a good job, all three of the children are first-class citizens. They're all married now, and Rebecca is a grandmother with a super set of grandchildren. "Such a blessing," she says, "I don't know what I'd do without them." Yes, it's a good report considering, and I am glad.

I am also glad for this note in her last letter:

I'm thinking of marriage again. Clyde is ten years older, a true Christian gentleman. Someday when we see each other again, I'll tell you how we met. It's almost unbelievable. You'll love it; I can just hear you saying, "That had to be an angel."

I think back sometimes to that terrible day when you came just as I was getting the news. I think *that* had to be an angel, too.

So do I, Rebecca. How else could I have gotten the message but by Divine intervention? I still don't understand the terrible side of it. Where was God when the wire broke?

Same questions. Same unknowns. But isn't this one great promise from our Lord?

> *"What I do thou knowest not now:*
> *But thou shalt know hereafter."*
> **John 13:7**

SIX

Babies, Children, and the Angels

"You know me, Charlie. I've always been one of the doubting-Thomas-types. But I tell you for sure when I held little Jason in my arms, my skepticism went smash. How could anyone go through all the feelings a baby brings without believing God is a miracle-worker? It really is awesome, isn't it, how the plan of God comes clear at a time like this? Why did Felicia and I go to the same school? Why did we marry each other instead of someone else? I know the answer now. There never would have been our particular little Jason if all those things hadn't happened. He's so absolutely perfect. There just had to be a whole lot of background planning to create him and bring him to Felicia and me. And I tell you something else, Charlie. You can talk about angels now all you want, because from this week on I'm a big believer."

One page from a five-page letter. One euphoric young father sharing his exuberance with his former pastor. The Bible says, "A little child shall lead them." And so shall a newborn baby.

What is the relationship between babies, angels, and children? Back to the Bible again and here's another exciting study waiting for us: Look up every place in Old Testament and New where angels had something to do with the little ones and the young. And how's this for a starter? "How many times in the Bible did an angel tell expectant parents what they should name their newborn child?"

Philip and the Hot Rod

*P*hilip was three, and always on the go. But he was very dependable. Every day he would get lost at least once. Ours was a small Nebraska village, and we lived near "downtown." A lumber yard and the fire station were on the way downtown, and those two places were usually number one and two on our check list. Philip loved them both, and the folks there returned his feeling—especially the firemen's Dalmatian.

Philip was a favorite at the lumber yard, too. Customers and staff made a pet of him. They bought him gum from the gumball machine and free soft drinks. When he got to be a nuisance, the nice bookkeeper would give us a ring.

It was a good arrangement for everyone, especially Philip. But this day we were ready for our evening meal and no Philip. After checking his usual haunts, we knew he had to be somewhere else, so we started our daily multi-search. Sometimes he'd be playing on the porches so we began there.

As we opened the front door there was Philip, but not on the porch. Instead, bent over in the middle of Main Street, our boy was examining something wonderful. A rock? The ants on bivouac? Somebody's old cigar? What a world he lived in. Everything on earth was worth attention—except for red cars bearing down on little boys. To them he paid no mind at all.

Is there any village so small it doesn't have at least one red car with a hot-rod driver? Ours was a nice kid, really. I knew him well. He came to our church youth group, and everyone liked him. He'd been reported frequently, paid any number of fines, and twice his license had been revoked.

Now there he was, roaring down the street full blast, headed straight for our little boy. We both screamed, loud. Which made not one little dent in Philip's scientific research. It also made not one bit of difference in the speed of the oncoming disaster. Of course we prayed. "Oh, God, no" is a form of prayer, isn't it?

Then suddenly, two or three car lengths from Philip, the hot rod came to a screeching halt. Dashing to pick up our precious son (more precious than ever, now), I gathered him in my arms and burst into tears.

At last when I had my breath—when I could think where I was and what to do next—I made my way to the red car. By now several other teenagers were gathered round, laughing, talking, being teens.

Moving into the driver's window I said, "Thank you, Kenny, for stopping in time. I was so afraid you would hit him. Thank you. Thank you."

"What do you mean? What are you talking about?"

"Didn't you see Philip right there in your path? Bent over. Looking at something in the street. Didn't you hear us scream?"

"Naw. I never saw nothin'. Never heard nothin'."

"Then why did you stop? All of a sudden you just stopped."

"Well, my buddy waved. That's why I stopped."

"Did any of you other guys see my little boy in the street? Right there in front of Kenny's car?"

"Nope. Didn't see a thing. Just Kenny. So we ran out to wave him down."

Then one of the more precocious members of the retinue said, "Lucky Kenny saw us wave, wasn't it?"

What is luck? The dictionary says luck is "the events or circumstances that operate for or against an individual." But wouldn't it be all right if we'd make that for or against a group? Like one toddler studying life at midstreet. Like one mom and one dad who could breathe again. Like the town hot rod, who really wasn't that bad and was certainly no killer. Like his buddies, spared their most horrible memory ever. Thank you, Lord, that this single event operated *for* and not *against* so many.

So define it any way you like and spell it any way that suits you. Luck. Chance. Fate. Irony. But looking back, I'll say, "Thank you, Lord, for one more brush of an angel's wing. Thank you that angels can use one buddy's wave to stop a car. Thank you also that one teenage hot rod saw those angelic waves and came to a screeching halt."

Thou art great and doest wondrous things.
Psalm 86:10

Ronnie and His Praying Church

*And you must think constantly about these commandments...
You must teach them to your children and talk about them when
you are at home or out for a walk; at bedtime and the first thing
in the morning... and write them on the doorposts of your
house.* Deuteronomy 6:6–8 TLB

"Vespers" was a service for the young from babies
up to college students. Every Sunday evening at
five o'clock they would come. They'd bring their friends,
and it was some gathering. Favorite hymns of the children, anthems by the children's choirs, baptisms often. A
time for prayer and prayer requests. And "Bible Story
Time" instead of "Sermon." Then the moments for questions and answers from the children, for the children.
Our bulletin notice read, "Parents are welcome at Vespers, provided they will *not* have anything to say at discussion time. (This notice written by the children.)"

Ronnie was always there with his mother, father, and two sisters. Ronnie was five, and this was the year he'd go to kindergarten. It would be a better kindergarten, too, because Ronnie was fun, had a big smile, everybody's friend.

Only this Sunday Ronnie wasn't there. Two sisters yes, but Walt and Helen, Ronnie's parents, weren't there either. They were at the hospital with a very sick Ronnie. It had come on him all at once and the doctors were puzzled. We had some excellent doctors in our town, and one of their major strengths was that when they didn't know what was wrong, they said so.

This time they'd all said so, and that meant a fast trip to the big city. Almost everybody in our town worked for the same company, and they had a company plane. Executive style, ready to go anywhere on call. But this I thought showed real class: on occasion, when someone was dangerously ill—company worker or not—away the plane would go, carrying one of our citizens.

I talked with Ronnie's mother that Sunday morning, and she said they still didn't know much. All kinds of tests with no diagnosis yet. I prayed with her by phone and assured her we'd be praying for them at all services, including Vespers. And we were.

Ronnie and his family had many friends, all highly concerned. We started this particular Vespers with a simple announcement telling what I knew, followed by a long period of silent prayer. Helen promised she'd call back if there was any change, any news at all.

And there was. At eight thirty that evening I answered

our home phone to one of the most jubilant voices I'd ever heard. It was Ronnie's mother.

"You're not going to believe it, but late this afternoon Ronnie sat up, said he was hungry, and asked to go home. When the nurses came they called the doctor. He took one look and asked, 'Whatever happened?' Then he began to examine Ronnie's blood pressure, heartbeat, temperature readings, everything. And the only thing he could figure was that maybe one of the powerful antibiotics finally got through."

Helen paused and then continued. "I told him, 'Doctor, the people in our church were praying for Ronnie today, including the children at Vespers.'"

She laughed. "Do you know what he did then? He turned around, gave me a long look and said, 'Guess the prayers got through too, didn't they? Would you tell them thanks for me?'"

Helen and I talked on for a long time. And then I asked, "Do you remember what time it was when Ronnie sat up and wanted to go home?"

"I certainly do," she answered, *"Wally and I were thinking about all of you praying at Vespers, so we were praying too. That would have been a little after five, wouldn't it?"*

Here's that question again. What did the angels have to do with Ronnie's amazing turnaround? Maybe nothing, but thinking it through: how many angels might have been serving the Lord behind scenes and where? Were they with the doctors who knew this problem needed expertise beyond their own skills? Humility is such a rare trait, and angels do have a way of keeping us humble. Were they with the company executives who first came up with the idea of using their executive plane for emergency medical needs? Angels can permeate the secular world too, can't they? And those saints of the church way back there who first thought up our Vespers? Who inspired them? Who helped them sell the idea of a service just for children? This could go on and on, couldn't it?

Lord, thank you for the brush of your angel's wings through so many people in so many places.

Karen and the Twins

*K*aren, our only daughter, age thirteen, was going on a trip. With her two best friends, the twins, and another buddy, they were ready. Destination, the beach at Galveston, a short afternoon drive down the freeway from Houston. The twins' parents' station wagon was one of those "fun" back seat jobs. *Would you like to see where you've been? Sit in the back, facing rear.*

"Let's draw straws. This time lucky Karen, lucky Janice." They win the rear seats, the other two girls up front. Beach bags packed, snacks aplenty, they are ready for take off.

Suddenly, for no apparent reason, Karen announced, "I can't go. I have to go home and help my mother."

"What's wrong, Karen? Are you sick?"

"Did somebody hurt your feelings?"

"We're going to have so much fun! Please come with us."

Still Karen would not change her mind, nor could she offer an explanation. Not sick. No hurt feelings. So to everyone's bewilderment including her mother's, she called home.

"But, Karen, you've already done your chores. I really don't need more help this afternoon. Something wrong? Are you sick? Did you have a fuss with your friends?"

"No, Mom, I just can't go. Please come get me."

All afternoon, Karen sat in her room listening to records. All afternoon her mother and I discussed the situation. Should we take her to the doctor? If so, what kind?

At last the station wagon headed for Galveston. Without Karen, all three girls faced forward. While the car inched along in bumper-to-bumper traffic, they talked about their friend's strange behavior.

Then it happened. Suddenly a chain reaction. Car crashing into car on the Galveston freeway. People screaming. People hurt. And where was the station wagon? You guessed it. Central in the smash up.

Comment from the highway patrol: "Sure a good thing nobody was riding in the back seat, folks. Somebody would have been killed."

A former Holy Land shepherd gives us a new look at the familiar Bible verse, "He restoreth my soul." This verse, he says, should be interpreted, "He turneth back my soul." The shepherd's staff has a crook on the end for several reasons. One is to turn the sheep back from danger. About to drink from poisoned water, about to plunge over a cliff, even a lamb may be "restored" to the safety of the flock. "Turned back" by the shepherd's crook.

Sidney and the Bull

Sidney was one of my best friends. We were neighbors out there in the country, and we often walked home from school together. Fifth grade buddies. Every afternoon when school let out we would poke along, throwing rocks, having fun. But one day I wasn't with Sidney, and he had an unforgettable experience. The big red bull went berserk. They do that sometimes when they decide school boys have had enough of their stomping ground.

So the bull started after Sidney and Sidney ran. That's a very good thing to do when a bull goes berserk. But it was a long way to the fence, and the bull ran faster than Sidney. Even though Sidney dropped every one of his books, the bull was gaining as they neared the gate. Knowing that this was the highest gate around, Sidney realized the awful truth. If he took time to climb, his chances of being gored were somewhere near a hundred percent. So he jumped. He took off and sailed over the gate.

There is nothing particularly unusual about a boy

being chased by an angry bovine. That must have happened thousands of times in the history of bulls and boys. But one day, out of curiosity, my friend Sidney and I went back and tried again to jump that particular gate. Yet try as we might, no way.

Some experts on human physiology make this claim: there are reserves in all of us we've never tapped. Powers we've never used, hidden ideas, countless good things waiting for release. Some say we use only fifty percent of our strength, our brains, our possibilities. Others say only ten percent.

Maybe they're right. Was it by coincidence that Sidney, when his legs were fully grown, went out for the track team? And did it just happen that he went on to break records in the high hurdles? Junior High. High School. College. On and on he went clearing those hurdles. Fast. High.

Lord, help us all to approach life's every challenge knowing you have equipped us with dormant energies and latent powers. And thank you, too, that some of your angels seem to deliver surges of power for escaping oil vats, ripping off car doors, and clearing high fences.

Jessica's Best Friends

Some girls at twelve are tall and thin, some still short and chubby. Then there are twelve-year-olds like Jessica Ann, just right. Beautiful red hair, beautiful smile. If you'd seen her that night you'd have said, "This must be what they mean by, 'A thing of beauty and a joy forever.'"

It was the after-meeting, dialogue time in a session on angels. They'd asked me to deal with the angel theme and, as usual, interest was high. We'd heard the reports of various people describing their extraordinary happenings. Fascinating stories and many questions.

As our time drew to a close, a dignified gentleman asked for the floor. Then, rather than speaking from his place, he came forward to address us.

"I've listened to everything every one of you has said here tonight," he began, "and I feel compelled to have my say. But you won't like it because the plain truth is that you are deluding yourselves. You are letting your imaginations run wild; some of you may even be hallucinating; and that goes for you, too, Dr. Shedd.

"I am a physician, and I came here tonight from another town hoping for some wisdom on the angel theme. Obviously I have drilled another dry hole. And that's how it always turns out. All my life I've listened to people's reports on extra-sensory perception and things like that. Every doctor dealing with the seriously ill gets it again and again. I've hoped sometime, somewhere, it would make sense, but it doesn't. So here I am, disappointed once more.

"In case you think I am anti-God, you should know that I go to church. I am on my church board. I tithe. I pray. I read my Bible. I have studied the Bible's angel stories, and I can only conclude the biblical writers were trying to tell us something which happened only way back then. Now really, wouldn't you think, if angels *were* real in our day, as a physician I would have had at least one experience I could credit to the Heavenly Host?

"So I can only say, if you folks are right then something is wrong with me. I did not believe in angels when I came here. I do not believe in angels now. Goodnight."

Then he turned and headed for the door. But just before he reached the exit, this lovely young redhead rose from her seat and said, "Doctor, will you wait a minute? I've listened to you. Please come back and listen to me."

He did. And this was what he heard.

"My name is Jessica Ann, and I am twelve years old. I am finishing sixth grade this month. Next year I'll be in junior high and I can hardly wait. I live with my mother because my father left us three years ago.

"My mother and I both know we'd never have made it without all the things angels have done for us since my dad left. Can you imagine what it is like when your mother doesn't even have a job and you wonder how you are going to make it?

"Well, she has a good job now, and if I had time I would tell you how an angel helped her get the job. When I was in an accident and they were afraid I would be scarred forever, we are sure it was an angel who didn't let that happen.

"There is so much more I could tell you about angels and what they do for us. They tell us what to do, where to go, what is right for us, and what isn't. I hope some day you will change your mind and know what my mother and I know. And this is one thing I know for sure. *The more you like angels, the more they will like you.* So maybe that's what's wrong. If you would try to be best friends with the angels—just once—maybe they would be best friends with you."

End of speech, end of story, and I am sorry that's the end. If only I'd gotten the doctor's name and address. If only I'd done the same with Jessica. I don't even know if the doctor was impressed, but you can be sure of this: Every one of us was not only impressed, we were awed. How could this beautiful near-teen be so mature, so sure of herself?

If you are an angel believer, I think you will agree:

Angels *can* do wonderful things for girls and their mothers; for other girls who know they must *not* go somewhere on a Sunday afternoon; for one little boy in the hospital and another running from a bull.

Good thought, Jessica: If I would try to be better friends with the angels, could they be better friends with me?

Angels and the Love Matches

In my years as a minister I have become convinced that there is an entire association of angels whose single work is bringing couples together.

"We knew the minute we met."

"I didn't even like him at first. But gradually something changed my mind, and I did a complete turnaround."

"I fell in love with her voice before I even saw her."

And on and on.

Of all the angel assignments, this group must include the most jokers, smilers, and designers. And I thank you, angels, that you can use the clergy too for romantic introductions.

From All-American to All-Martha

*H*er voice was like a song, and considering her subject, that was surprising. She was reading history. "Important dates," the teacher said. Important people too, plus places important. But why should I care? I didn't like girls.

The little community where I grew up had several things going for it. But none better than the school possibilities for eighth graders. We could choose any one of four high schools. We were an unincorporated village with no educational loyalty. So which would it be: East Waterloo, West Waterloo, Cedar Falls, or Teacher's College High?

For those of us on the eighth-grade football team, there was no debate. Every year West Waterloo finished strong, often winning state championships. Every year their best made all-state. Some would be offered scholarships to Big Ten schools. A few in West High's history had even gone to the pros.

For me there was no question. I would go to West Waterloo. All-Big Ten. All-American. All-pro. All-Charlie.

In early June that summer, the town of Cedar Falls annexed our little village, and there went my choices. I was to enroll in the nearest school, and that meant Cedar Falls High. No one could remember their last winning season.

What do we do when our hopes come crashing down? Despair in junior high may not be worse than despair at any other age. Perhaps it only *seems* worse. For me, this was the lowest blow of all the world's low blows that summer.

So off I went to Cedar Falls High at a slow shuffle, pouting all the way.

It was a huge question on the eighth-grade level: "Why would God do me this way? Me! Future all-Big Ten, all-American, all-pro,… all-done-in-with-despair. How *could* he?"

Football season was opening Friday night. We'd been practicing for three weeks. Before school started, the coach had been shaping us up. I was looking out the classroom window, wondering: "Will I be in the starting lineup? Freshmen usually sit on the bench, but maybe I'll have a chance. We need bulk in the line, and I am bulky."

Then I heard a voice—a voice like a song. She was wearing yellow. Big yellow sweater, yellow skirt. There was an aura about her I'd never seen on any girl before —and a new sound, too. What is this in all that data she is reading? It was supposed to be history, but surely it was more. A background song? A soul song? An angelus with the one word title *Charlie?*

We were in several classes together, and as I studied her, I picked up an interesting ritual. Always before the "class-come-to-order-now" bell, she would go to the teacher's desk and sharpen her pencil. I liked that. Be prepared, and especially, be sharp.

Not being skilled in the ways of first love, I pondered an approach. And how was this for an amateur? At home I scrounged for dull pencils, and every day joined her at the pencil sharpener.

During our early pencil sharpening together, we stumbled around for some mutual interests. Then we found our theme. She liked to ice skate, and so did I. Most Iowa teens skated well because we skated often, and we skated for many reasons. Reason one for us right now was "boys and girls together."

Washington Pond was big, with smooth ice, beautiful overhanging trees, and a huge bonfire to warm ourselves. There were also miscellaneous coves for those who warmed better with a little privacy. *Let's find a private bower, Charlie, so we can visit, visit, visit.*

When summer came, I was ready. From Manual Training class I'd learned exactly what I needed now: "How to Build a Rowboat." So I built one. Solid, easy rowing, painted yellow. Yellow was her favorite color, I was her favorite fellow, and this was our favorite river. So off we would go in my boat to find another private cove. Idyllic. Romantic. Even the birds that summer were singing our favorite songs. But that's not all. How many times those five, six, seven winters and summers of our courtship did it happen? We would feel the touch of an angel's wing and know—God had sent someone straight from heaven to teach us, guide us, protect us, and blend these two hearts for him.

Football? Oh yes, there was a game named football, wasn't there? And hadn't I heard something way back there about a frivolous goal called all-American? But why should such trivia bother me?

From that time on I was all-Martha,
all-everything to her,
and she all-everything to me.
Absolutely, one hundred percent, "Angelic."

Love Match at the Crystal Cathedral

We were in Dr. Schuller's study, top floor, Crystal Cathedral. It is an amazing house of the Lord. Stone and glass in the California sun. I was talking on the phone to my old friend Lawrence Johnson. Old? Depends on your label for "old." Eighty years is not old if you're "old" like Lawrence Johnson. For many years we were fellow workers, sharing the deepest of friendships.

But during this particular phone call, were we talking about our years together in the ministry? No, we were talking about the woman Martha and I had found for Lawrence.

Before you think we were in a mail-order bride business, tune your heart to my explanation.

Houston, Texas was a throbbing city in the early 60s—oil center, international shipping center, space center. Hundreds of new people moving to Houston daily. And on a strategic corner of all this growth, the newly organized Memorial Drive Presbyterian Church would be built. We needed help. Two thousand members in five years and growing much too fast. Certainly too fast for one pastor. So I invited Lawrence to come from Oklahoma and help us. He was exactly the kind of help we needed. Visit the members, visit the newcomers, visit the sick and the well. Let them know somebody cares, "Somebody loves you."

When I resigned this big church for a smaller one to give myself writing time, Lawrence stayed on. At the time of this story, he was working in another important position. Five days each week, eight hours each day, he was minister to out-of-town Presbyterians at the mammoth Houston Medical Center.

Lawrence and his wife, Elizabeth, were approaching their 50th anniversary. For a long time she had not been well, and she was hurting. "Charlie," she confided in me, "I'm going to hang on for our golden wedding celebration, and then I'll go." And that's exactly what she did. Lawrence became a lonesome widower.

After four years of living by himself, one day Lawrence made an unusual phone call to share a most extraordinary decision. "Charlie," he began, "I'm lonesome. I want to be married again, and I have a plan. Since you're my very best friend, I'd like to check it with you."

Then Lawrence outlined his plan, and it was, indeed, extraordinary. He would go back to some of his former parishes and visit. Especially he would visit certain widows, women who, with their husbands, had been among his best friends.

"What do you think?" he asked. My reply was exactly what you would reply to a friend most extraordinary. "Go for it!" So he went.

But, in biblical parlance, "He returned empty-handed." Still no companion. Still lonely.

Martha and I were going to the Crystal Cathedral that summer. I was preaching for Dr. Schuller while he was on vacation. Before we left, Lawrence phoned with another extraordinary proposal.

"Charlie, dear friend," he began as usual. "Out there in the Crystal Cathedral I understand you'll be preaching to eight thousand people. Somewhere among them, shouldn't there be one fine lady exactly right for me? Please, when you get settled, will you two look around and maybe make some inquiries?"

How could any real friend do anything other than act on a request like that? So we acted. The first day we arrived in California, Martha and I went to Dr. Schuller's office. His secretary had written that she would be glad to help us any way she could. Nice offer. Nice lady. We planned to share our mission with her, tell her about Lawrence and what we were looking for.

There must be a special place in heaven for pastors' secretaries. They've heard it all, seen it all, done it all. And if they haven't done it all, they can probably devise some way to do it. They love challenges, and Barbara took this challenge.

As we were about to leave her office, we said, "Think it over. We'll be back later for names and information."

"I'll do my best," she promised. Then suddenly a light came on. "Wait a minute," she said, "I know the lady you're looking for. She's my mother-in-law! She'd be absolutely perfect. Love, nothing but love. Cute, big smile, smart, and she's only seventy! Her name is Helen. She's lonesome, too. Yes. Yes. Yes. She'd be exactly right for your preacher friend."

Martha smiled, "I'll take her for lunch tomorrow and check her out."

When they came back from lunch the next day, I was waiting in The Hour of Power Tower. As Martha passed me at the door she whispered, "Give her an A plus!"

So there I was on Dr. Schuller's private phone, passing the good news to Lawrence. "Come," I said. "Come on your way to Alaska." (He had booked himself for a tour.) But Lawrence, ever the careful planner, hesitated. "I'll call you back." And he did. "I can't do it, Charlie. I checked with my travel agent, and it'll cost me too much money to stop by California."

"Lawrence," I cajoled, "how could a man as smart as you are be so utterly obtuse? When you are eighty years old, what are a few extra dollars to meet the next Mrs. Johnson?"

Moment of silence. Then, "Of course. You're right, Charlie. I'll be there."

So he was there and we were there and Helen was

there. All of us meeting at the airport. As Lawrence de-planed, we sensed it right away. In what seemed a matter of seconds, we knew and he knew and she knew—*this was it!*

They have been married for fifteen years now. Lawrence, ninety-four, has recently retired as Chaplain at Houston Medical Center. "Why would you do that, Lawrence? Couldn't you work those few more years till you reach your century mark?"

To which, always the same warm answer. "When you love each other as much as Helen and I do, you really need more time to love each other. You also need time to travel. Don't you know, Helen has never quit reminding me that I owe her a trip to Alaska. Do you think she really expected me to invite her along to Alaska on our very first date?"

"Yes," I answer, "I think she did. Watching you together, almost anyone would think so."

Questions, questions:

Were Martha and I at the Crystal Cathedral that summer only to preach for Dr. Schuller?

Why did we go first to Dr. Schuller's secretary?

How many daughters-in-law could recommend their mother-in-law without equivocation?

Why was Lawrence heading for Alaska, making an easy stop in California?

If we would make ourselves more available for God's linking people to people, would he use us more often in his Happy Surprises?

And how many angels do you suppose were involved in all these intricate machinations bringing two together for a long-time love?

So right for us, aren't they, these words of Proverbs 3:6:

> *In all thy ways acknowledge him,*
> *and he shall direct thy paths.*

Prevenient Grace

"Prevenient"—an old theological term.
In its original, it meant simply "ahead of time."
God's love ahead of time.

An angel at the tomb said,
"Lo, he goeth before you."

The secret is to make sure that I am following him
rather than urging him to follow me.

"Come on, Lord, this is one of my busy days.
So much to do. Hurry. Hurry."

But all the while, God goes at his own pace, doing
    things the way he knows they should be done.
When will I ever learn to pray and mean it,
"You go first, Lord. I'll follow."

The Years which the Locust Hath Eaten

$\mathcal{M}$y second pastorate was in Nebraska—seven hundred members and much, much too large a congregation for a young pastor three years out of seminary. But I was called there, and I think they knew somehow they'd taken a boy to raise. They were loving, enthusiastic, fun. And, being farmers, they kept our freezer full of hind quarters, front quarters, and things in between.

A wise old preacher and member of the Nebraska church family told me: "Son, no matter how smart you become, you will never know as much as the Bible. So every week, pick out some text you like, and do your best. If you do that, most of the people will get something from even your poorest effort."

Thank you, caring friend. Your advice was, and still is, right on target. The Word of the Lord does have an impact I could never have on my own. Like the day of the happy surprise in Barmore's drug store (open every day, including Sunday).

This is a story of one of my failures. By my standards, it was a failure, but God had a bigger plan. That's how it often is in his prevenience—love ahead of time.

For my text that Sunday, I had chosen Joel 2:25: "I will restore unto you the years which the locust hath eaten." Not much background in the passage, really. However, I did like it, and wasn't "like it" where my elderly mentor had told me to start? Yet somehow, though I honestly tried, it simply wouldn't preach. For me, the poor thing fell with a dull thud.

I could tell that even Martha had her doubts. When we sat down to her customary Sabbath spread, things were not like our Sunday noon custom. Her usual "I think you're wonderful" smile was a bit subdued. So we discussed my feelings and her feelings. Then we decided together we should put this week's feeble effort out of its misery. We did. With a special prayer for that kind of misery, we laid it away.

Only it wouldn't stay away. All afternoon it would push over the tombstone and leer at me. Fortunately, it was a busy Sunday and busyness is good balm for sore memories. But there is another balm I like. On my way home I decided a thick Barmore milkshake was exactly what I needed. I call this "Comfort me with something creamy."

Fred Barmore was one of our elders. Good man. Good friend. He must have recognized the downward thrust of my spirits so he made the shake that Sunday exactly like I loved his shakes—extra size, extra sweet, extra thick. Delicious. Super soothing.

Halfway through this sin of the flesh, Fred remembered something. Suddenly he got up from the table where we sat visiting and ran to the cash register.

"There was a couple in church this morning from Ogalalla. Nice folks. They stopped here for a sandwich. And when they left, they gave me this envelope to give you first time I saw you."

If I were to list on five fingers the most beautiful letters ever to come my way, this one would surely be included.

Dear Reverend Shedd:

We are from Ogalalla and on our way to Lincoln. Since we always go to church, we stopped today for your service.

There is no way we could tell you what your sermon meant to us. Actually, we were heading for Lincoln to consult a lawyer friend. Sorry to say we were going to work out details for a divorce. We had both decided our marriage was hopeless.

But here we sit in this drugstore having lunch, and as we waited for our order something happened we think you should know. We began discussing those simple little rules you gave for restoring a marriage the locust had been chewing on so long. The more we talked the more we knew the Lord had been speaking to us through you, so this is what we decided to do. Instead of heading for Lincoln, we're heading back home to begin restoring what was once a wonderful love. Thank you.

Why did they happen to be going through our town at everybody's church hour? Did they feel the brush of an angel's wing guiding them our way? Ours is the God who rescues failures. By angel or whatever the method. That's exactly what he promised in the morning text, isn't it? It's a great promise.

I will restore unto you the years which the locust hath eaten.
Joel 2:25

Do Not Move
Forward Alone

*I*n the mountains of Thailand, there is a little village where the entire population was converted in one great revival. Unfortunately, upon their conversion these people were confronted with a major problem. Their mountain territory was and is a major grower of opium. It is the base of their entire economy.

Being converted to Christianity was more than a wonderful change of heart for them. It threatened their single source of livelihood. They decided to convert their plantings to vegetables and garden products. Great idea, except for one thing. The only transportation they had for their produce is pack horse, or horse-drawn cart down the mountain.

Another problem. Their vegetables and fruits were ripe for delivery during the monsoon seasons. And though the rain was not a major problem for the people, it was for horses. Too many of the horses, unaccustomed to such heavy work in this kind of weather, died on their way to market.

So they reached out to their Baptist sponsors for help. If only there might be someone, somewhere, who could provide some mule jacks for breeding to their horses.

Mules are much tougher than horses for some purposes. And there is no other way to produce a mule than by breeding a mule jack to a horse.

Through a friend at the American Bible Society, we heard their story. Perfect project for us.* Cutting through a maze of red tape, we finally had our project approved. At last we could import some mammoth mule jacks from Australia to the little village in Thailand.

Several years later we went to Thailand, hoping to visit our mules high up the mountains. But when we arrived, someone had placed a humble sign at the foot of the road. Actually, it's little more than a walking trail, but it's their road and their sign.

"DO NOT MOVE FORWARD ALONE
DUE TO UNFORTUNATE MURDER MAYBE"

Was it a joke? Someone trying to be clever? Why the quaint wording? We did not understand, but we weren't about to "move forward alone" without some serious in-

---

* Publisher's Note: Since the publication of Dr. Shedd's best selling books, *Letters to Karen* and *Letters to Philip*, one half of his royalties have been designated for "The Abundance Foundation." This is a foundation established for hunger relief and dedicated to the purchase of animals to assist in agricultural missions.

quiry. So we began knocking on doors. First, we wanted to find out the story behind the sign. More than that, we must find the missionary responsible for our involvement in the mule project.

Angel One had been working behind the scene. A little old man ran a small stand where we first stopped to inquire. Yes, he knew a "leetle" English. No, he did not know the missionary, but he did have a Christian friend. Maybe his friend would know how we might find the missionary. "I send for him. He come." And the friend came. Happy surprise. The little man's friend said, "Your friend, he my friend. He move Hong Kong. Maybe you find him Hong Kong."

The population of Hong Kong is five million. We were still in Thailand, and we needed to locate one missionary among five million people. One missionary, unfortunately with a common name.

The hospitality lady at our hotel gave us good advice: Call Hong Kong Long Distance Information. Tell your operator who you're trying to find, and she will connect you with "Special Assistance."

Angel Two also working back stage. We connected with the long distance operator in Hong Kong. When we told a sweet little oriental voice who we were looking for, there was a long silence. Then in great excitement she said, "Oh, I know him! He wonderful man. Sometime he preach my church. Thank you. I ring him for you."

She did and now another miracle of timing. "I'm so glad you called today," the missionary responded. "Monday my family and I are leaving for the States. We'll be six months on furlough. Can you come immediately?

We'll show you Hong Kong. Please come."

Of course we accepted and it was one great time. So many fascinating behind-the-scenes places. So many interesting explanations. Including details on the road sign to our mule project. "Opium is the main crop up there in the mountains," he said, "and they allow no visitors. None. That sign was painted by an old man who loves you for your gift to the mission. He was protecting you from danger."

"You simply cannot believe what your mule jacks have done. The Christians are still raising vegetables and still carrying them to market with your mules. In only five years that little village has raised enough mules to share with any number of other villages wanting to do what they've done. As a matter of fact, they have a word which could never be translated in English but it means something like, 'Mules sent by the Lord.'"

The extraordinary happenings of how many angels?

A caring little sign-painter up our mountain who may have saved our lives.

That man at the wayside stand and his friend who knew our missionary.

One Christian operator we needed. Out of hundreds and hundreds of long distance operators in Hong Kong, *the* one for us.

So many extraordinary happenings in one journey.

But why not? Isn't ours the extraordinary God who goes before us?

It really is one holy combination of words, isn't it? The sign for any trip, anytime—

DO NOT MOVE FORWARD ALONE!

Whether you turn to the right or to the left,
your ears will hear a voice behind you, saying,
'This is the way; walk in it.'
Isaiah 30:21

Andrew and the Diving Coach

*M*y fourteen-year-old stepson is "on the outs" with me, meaning very much "put off." He is also down in spirit, way down. He has come now to visit me in Austin, Texas, coming to have a look at his new home.

I have accepted a position on the preaching staff at Riverbend Church. One of America's fastest growing mega-churches, Riverbend needs help. So I am here waiting for Diane and Andrew to join me. Moving date for them is still a few weeks distant, so Andrew has come to look things over. And Andrew is brokenhearted. He is leaving his girlfriend, leaving his ninth grade buddies, leaving his baseball teammates. Football; basketball; hanging out; all kinds of fun. Leaving.

Pronto, out of the airplane, he begins his litany: "Why are you doing this to me, Charlie?" New school, new church, new city, new malls, nothing impressed him. All plain "dumb." "Why are you doing this to me?" and off we go again.

I have been sleuthing a bit before he arrives, nosing about for some young folks Andrew's age. Would they please come see him while he's here? Of course, they would be glad to. Especially the girls would be glad to. So here they are, three young lovelies to take him swimming.

Andrew has always had a thing for diving. Since he was two, he's loved the water and especially diving. Training? No. Just watch the TV divers and do what they do. Even without training he is a beautiful diver, and I was awed as I watched him.

Abruptly a tall, attractive lady sat down beside me. As she watched, she asked, "Who is this boy? How old is he? Who does he train with?"

"His name is Andrew. Andrew is fourteen. He's my stepson, and he's never trained with anyone. He simply likes to dive."

"Andrew, come here," she called. "Do you know how good you are, son? I have never seen a fourteen-year-old dive like you dive. I'm the coach at this pool, and I'm here because the lifeguards called me. 'Come see this boy dive,' they said. 'You won't believe it.' And they were right, Andrew. If I hadn't seen it I wouldn't believe it." Etcetera for sometime. Truly a speech to soothe the broken-hearted teenager.

Then she told him that every year the University of

Texas coaches select a few high schoolers from all the schools in Austin for special training. Each day, after school, they go to the University Swimming Center. "Probably the finest in America, Andrew. And there they are, training under the greatest coaches in the world. And do you know why? They're training future divers for the University of Texas. No wonder, is it, that Texas is always way up there in national competition? And international. They travel all over the world: Europe, Spain, the Orient."

"I can guarantee, Andrew, absolutely guarantee, that you can be one of the chosen. Right away, no waiting. Then, by the time you graduate from high school, you'll be on scholarship competing with the very best. Oh, and don't forget about the next Olympics."

I watched as Andrew listened and what did I see? The miracle. One hundred percent reversal from hurting anger to soaring hope: "I, Andrew, can become a national, international, University of Texas, full scholarship, Olympic diver!!"

Why had I accepted an invitation to preach for an extended period at an exciting church in Austin, Texas? Why are so many champion divers trained in Austin? Why did these three girls take Andrew to this particular pool? Why were those particular guards, members of the high school team, on duty that particular day? "We wouldn't think of doing some of the dives he's doing," they said. Why was the coach free at the particular moment they called her, urging her to come? "Lucky I was home," she said. "I just got in from a weekend trip."

And one more question, this time from a differing perspective: Why were the three girls members of their church Bible study group for high schoolers? And why were they meeting in a home nearby that very night? "Will you come, Andrew? You'll meet a whole bunch of neat people."

Now back home with me. "How'd you do at the meeting, Andrew?"

"Awesome. Great kids." One hundred eighty degree turn around. Smile on his face, hope in his heart, let's get on with it; university champion diver, national, international champion too. Hallelujah!

Isn't it breathtaking, how the Divine Manager of All-Things-Wonderful choreographs his Happy Surprises? God's angels work as invisible weavers in the tapestry of our lives. And what beautiful designs unfold when we follow.

> *Man's life is laid in the loom of time*
> *To a pattern he does not see,*
> *While the weavers work*
> *… and the shuttles fly*
> *Till the dawn of eternity.*
> Unknown

New Friends from My Home Town

*H*awaii, 3:00 A.M. We have just disembarked from one of those planes seating four hundred. Now all four hundred of us are milling about in one big room. Our plane is refueling and that, the officials tell us, will take one hour. "Sorry we had to do this, folks, but you are locked in. Stretch yourselves, have a seat, get acquainted. Before you know it, we'll return to the plane and on to Australia." Which being interpreted means "You're tired, you're stiff, and we're only halfway."

Australia is a strikingly different place to vacation, but getting there by night is strikingly awful. Why do plane seats seem smaller and smaller and airline food worse and worse the further you travel?

"Have a seat," they say. So let's sit awhile. But where? Surely there must be four hundred seats for four hundred people. If that's true, where are the two for us? Suddenly we see two seats, four rows over, but hurry. Others have spotted them, too.

So here we are sitting in two more uncomfortable seats. What can passengers do now to ease the discomfort? Why not strike up a conversation with someone sitting near?

The address tags on people's luggage have always had a strange fascination for me. This time I can hardly believe what I am seeing. In plain view, jumping up and down beside me, the tag reads, Department of Home Economics, University of Northern Iowa, Cedar Falls, Iowa. Marilyn Storey, Department Head." I do a double take, then two or three more.

Cedar Falls, Iowa, is my hometown. I played football at UNI one year and my Martha graduated from the Home Economics Department there. This simply can't be. Four hundred of us in this miserable room. Hawaii. Far out in the Pacific and I am seated by someone from Cedar Falls.

"Pardon me, Ma'am, but I just happened to notice your luggage tag. Are you really from Cedar Falls, Iowa?"

"Yes."

"And you're head of the Home Economics Department at UNI?"

"Yes."

"That's incredible. Cedar Falls, Iowa is my hometown."

I give her my name, and from that moment it's celebrate, celebrate. I introduce Diane, and Marilyn introduces her husband. Norman is currently head of the Counseling Department at UNI. Suddenly the dull stupor of the long trip distills into a lively friendship. Hometowners sharing and caring and getting acquainted. And, taking care of some business. There is a trust in the Home

Economics Department of UNI in honor of Martha. And Marilyn wants me to know about the girls on scholarship from her trust.

Have you ever had occasions when time suddenly switches to fast forward? That's exactly how it seemed for the four of us.

I give Norman my card and he gives me his. Now as he reads my address, it's his turn for a quick retake.

"Georgia?" he asks, "Athens, Georgia? Do you happen to know where Hartwell is?"

"Of course we know Hartwell. One of the most beautiful lakes in the South. Only forty miles from our house. We love Lake Hartwell."

"Well, we do, too. We love it so much we're building our new home at Hartwell. We're both retiring and we'll be moving soon to the lake at Hartwell."

The call comes for us to reboard, and as we move along Norman says, "Just today we were speculating how we would make new friends in Georgia. Think of it. At a stopover in Hawaii. Unbelievable."

Four future neighbors traveling the same plane to Australia. Two vacant seats out of four hundred. One little piece of hand luggage with one little nameplate.

How could all this have happened way out here in the Pacific? For those of us who believe, there is only one answer: *"The Lord shall guide thee continually"* (Isaiah 58:11).

Continually. From Nebraska to Texas, Thailand to the Crystal Cathedral, Cedar Falls to Hartwell. Preparing the way ahead of time. From the past to this moment to off there in the distance. Isn't this the full meaning of these two beautiful words "Prevenient Grace?"

I believe in a loving God whose angels are never far away. And if I let them, they will guide me to those I should meet for his purposes.

Dreams and the Angels

For God speaks again and again,
in dreams, in visions of the night
when sleep falls on men as they lie on their beds.
He opens their ears in times like that.

Job 33:14–16 TLB

Again and again the Bible tells us that God comes to his
people in dreams. From Job and many others we have

this witness. Day, night, evening, early morning, any-time. With direction, assurance, comfort, advice, warn-ing, or tidings of great joy he comes. And how many times will his dream message come by angel? Many.

Does every dream arrive with an important message? Some say, "Yes." I have read writers, listened to speakers, and in discussion heard others who answer in the affir-mative. Yet here is one veteran dreamer who says other-wise. I believe that many of my dreams are gifts of the Lord for pure entertainment.

Then there are other like the little white note in Copen-hagen.

"Attention!
You are about to receive an important message.
This one straight from your caring Heavenly Father.

Or, depending on heavenly circumstance, your mes-sage may come from your caring Heavenly Father by way of a caring angel."

Little White Note in Copenhagen

Wolfsburg, Germany, is an exciting city. The city of Volkswagens—five thousand daily. The Scripture says, "Let everything be done decently and in order." That's how they do it in Wolfsburg. System. Smooth.

We were on a thirty-day tour of Europe, and we had come to Wolfsburg to buy a Volkswagen for our high-school son. This was Peter's graduation present, pre-ordered, everything exactly the way he wanted it. Color right. Accessories right. And oh, that Volkswagen welcome to Wolfsburg!

We stayed in one of those spotless German *pensions*—feather beds, plus breakfast, at bargain rates. It was here I dreamed an unusual dream. This one was about Grandma. My mother-in-law was extra-special. She liked me, too. What I liked most about her were the reflections of God I saw in her. Having already given me her daughter, she did another fine thing. She kept giving me the feeling that life with the Lord was one hundred percent natural.

It was Wednesday, July 21. In my dream we had arrived in Copenhagen, and there was a message. Grandma had died, and we must return to the States. The most vivid part of my dream was Peter in his little Volkswagen. It seemed to weave its way in and out of the dream, past the red cows and white barns, through the little towns, up and down the pleasant hills of Denmark and Germany, then to Amsterdam for return shipment.

The next morning I told the dream to Martha. Sometime back we had agreed to tell each other our dreams. And was I ever glad I'd told her this one!

That night at dinner in Hamburg I felt the nudge to share it with our boys. Timothy, our youngest, didn't like it. But with the typical "wisdom" of parenthood, we assured him it was only a dream. It took Peter, with the greater wisdom of youth, to say, "But Tim, Grandma is eighty-one. Let's face it. She's going to die sometime." So each of us put it on the shelf with things to be forgotten.

Friday we had a fascinating time in Grandma's hometown. At twenty-one she had come from Odense, Denmark, to the Midwest and Iowa. We had dinner with her relatives, visited St. Knud's Church where she had been baptized, and looked for the homes where she'd grown up. They were still there, in excellent shape. Her father was a carpenter.

Saturday we arrived in Copenhagen and reported to our travel agent. We had put the dream away, but not very far.

On our arrival at the hotel, Tim headed for the desk.
The rest of us stood in line to cash checks. There are
some moments to be remembered forever. One of mine
came when Tim handed me this note:

Important. Call Mr. Petersen, Portland, Oregon, immediately.

Then his number, and that was all.

Mr. Petersen is my brother-in-law. The four of us
looked at each other without a word. We went to our
room, placed the call, and it was exactly as we knew it
would be.

"Charlie, I'm sorry to tell you that Mom died this
morning. Pastor Tange said she ate a hearty breakfast,
then went to her room, and died."

For a long time we sat there sharing our feelings. We
cried. We prayed. Especially we thanked God for three
days of preparation by way of "our" dream.

Martha, Tim, and I took off the next morning on a
return flight. It was an intense moment as we watched
our eighteen-year-old drive away in his Volkswagen. Of
course, he made it safely past the red cows and white
barns, through the little towns, and over the gentle hills
to Amsterdam. Then he flew on to Iowa to meet us for
the funeral. Eighteen-year-olds can do so much more
than we as parents are prone to believe. Martha had
said, "Shouldn't one of us go with Peter?" To which he
observed, like the philosopher he is, "Mom, I'll do anything to make you feel better. If you want Dad to go with
me, that's fine. But wouldn't it spoil the dream?"

They have the nicest custom at Grandma's church. After the funeral, everyone comes together in the parlor for coffee, which for Danish people also means sandwiches of infinite variety, cookies of infinite variety, cakes of infinite variety, conversation of infinite variety.

I found myself talking with some of Grandma's special friends. I learned that she had been worried about our itinerary. We had asked our travel agent to send it to each member of our family, but she hadn't received her copy. Someone down the line had directed it to the wrong town; it arrived two days after her death.

"Do you suppose she asked the Lord to get in touch with you? She hadn't been feeling quite up to par. I wonder if she sensed something," one of her friends commented.

"You don't think that's impossible, do you?" Bertel answered. Bertel and his wife were two of Grandma's favorites. They took her to church on Sunday and for special events. "I don't think that's any harder to believe than your dreaming it before it happened," he said. "In fact, knowing Marie and how she lived with the Lord, I think that's exactly what happened. She asked him to look you up, and he did."

On the day we left home for our trip to Denmark, Martha had done something very unusual—she had written her brother a note. They had the best of feelings for each other, but they also had one of those relationships for which that's enough. They did have great times when they were together, but other than that, they loved each other in silence. Yet for some reason she felt compelled that day to send him this message: "We will be at Five Swans Hotel in Copenhagen on July 24."

There were nineteen known stops on our thirty-day schedule. These were confirmed reservations. The rest were of the do-it-yourself variety. In the three days prior to Grandma's death, we were free-floating through Germany and Denmark. The day following we were to board ship for three days' incommunicado sailing along the coasts of Sweden and Norway.

Why had she died that particular day? Why had Martha selected that particular stop to tell her brother? Why had we been given three days' notice by the dream? What is the explanation? How do we solve these mysteries?

There is only one answer. God in his love cares about us. He knows what we need to know. He knows where we need to be. It is not ours to push or crowd or hurry. Ours is to respond, follow his lead, and listen for his whispers.

Two Josephs and
Many Dreams

Joseph and The Amazing Technicolor Dreamcoat, is the title of a current smash hit on Broadway. No question about this, the Old Testament Joseph has always held a special fascination for those of us who love drama and the unusual. And this Joseph is one of the prominent characters whose life was guided by dreams.

A careful study of Joseph, son of Jacob, shows him to be a young man of high integrity. What Bible lover could ever forget his classic answer to Potiphar's wife? "How then can I do this great wickedness, and sin against God?" (Genesis 39:9 KJV).

Interesting, isn't it, that a New Testament Joseph takes center stage when we reflect on dreams and the angels? Why did the angels come so often to this Joseph? We are not left to wonder long. Three verses carry the clear and certain answer.

Behold, the angel of the Lord appeared unto him in a dream.... Then Joseph being raised from sleep *did as the angel of the Lord had bidden him.*   Matthew 1:20, 24 KJV

The angel of the Lord appeareth to Joseph in a dream, saying, "Arise, and take the young child and his mother, and flee."... *When he arose, he took the young child and his mother by night.*   Matthew 2:13–14 KJV

But when Herod was dead, behold, an angel of the Lord appeareth in a dream to Joseph saying, "Arise and take the young child and his mother, and go into the land of Israel."... *And he arose and took the young child and his mother and came into the land of Israel.*
Matthew 2:19–21 KJV

Three times angels came to this Joseph in a dream. Three time he acted immediately on the angel's instruction. Two words for me, you, anyone who would experience the frequent brush of an angel's wing:

Prompt Obedience!

Kinship with All Life

The cattle upon a thousand hills… horses bridled or running free… the ass who talked and foxes in their holes… snakes and other creeping things… the great fish of Jonah's story; a boatload of fish from casting on the other side… two small fish Jesus took to feed a multitude… the dove sent out by Noah, and ravens feeding a frightened prophet… even one sparrow which falleth not but that our heavenly Father knoweth.

God holds the whole world in his hand... the universe and everything in it—all his. And sometimes he even uses animals, birds and fish too, as traffic ways for his angels.

For me, it was one mule colt, one little cat, one suffering seagull, each with a message. And the message is this holy fact embedded in Scripture: All the universe and everything in it was made by him and for him to glorify His Holy name.

The Grateful Seagull

$\mathcal{G}$ulls look so beautiful in flight, in diving for food, in flocks following shrimp boats. But any seaman will tell us another thing about gulls: they may have an ugly disposition and may be vicious when cornered. With their feet and beak they can rip and tear to great destruction. *Never try to pet a gull. Never feed a gull. Stay away from gulls.* Quotes from beach signs.

Martha and I knew about gulls. We had observed the warnings at the beach, heard stories of gulls hurting people, read it in the seaside papers. We had also seen the angry gulls battle each other. Yes, we knew these birds were not for human handling. But what should we do about this poor gull?

Today as we walked the beach, we came upon him tangled in a piece of shrimpers' net. Angry at the net, angry at his fate, angry, angry. What would you do if you found a wounded gull on your beach, caught fast in a net? What would you do if you wanted to help, but your inner computer was thoroughly tracked with the warnings: *Do not approach, Never touch,* and *Stay away from wounded seagulls?*

As you would do, we prayed. But when we said "Amen," he was still caught in the net. Could he (or was he a "she"?) possibly understand that we were friends? Should we give it a try, attempt the rescue?

We did. Approaching the gull we said, "Gull, this will be hard for you to understand, but please try. We want to set you free. And if you will let us, one of us will pick you up while the other untangles the net. It won't be easy for you, and it won't be easy for us. It'll take awhile. But if we could be friends for whatever time it takes, we will be glad and so will you." With that our gull actually seemed to relax and we moved closer. I lifted the bird to my lap. Carefully, slowly, Martha began to untie knots and pull strings. All the while I was soothing the bird as best I could: quoting Bible verses, talking softly, assuring him.

Finally, wings loosed and freed at last, the gull flew out to sea. How good that must have felt to the gull. How good it felt to us. Then suddenly, as if from somewhere in its best gull self, it remembered its seagull manners.

Back it flew and called to us.

"What are you saying, gull?" Of course we couldn't be certain. Yet ever after, when our minds turned back to that day with the tangled gull, one of us would say, "Sure sounded like 'thank you,' didn't you think?" And the other would say, "I thought it rather sounded like, 'Thank you very much, and God bless you.'"

The Bible says "Love conquers all things." Could it possibly be that there is a message of love which rises above words to connect the human and the wild? The Scriptures affirm:

Ask the wild birds—they will tell you....
this is the Eternal's way."
Job 12:7, 9 (Moffatt)

Hawley Moses

*H*awley Memorial Presbyterian Church at Blue Ridge Summit, Pennsylvania, stands high on the Appalachian Mountains. It stands high on my list of favorite churches, too. We watched it grow from a sad church about to close its doors to a thriving congregation. My last Palm Sunday there I preached on Jesus' donkey ride. Couldn't he have found something more classy for his triumphal entry? Interesting theme. I liked it, and the people liked it, too. My congregation knew that I was an animal lover. They were not surprised when I said, "Someday, when I retire, I hope to become close friends with a donkey or a mule of my own."

Now this you will have a hard time believing, so try to put away your doubt while I give it to you true. On our last Sunday this congregation had an all community picnic. Band, balloons, smorgasbord, people, people, people. And then the time arrived for their going-away gift. Down the street came Herb, our Amish farmer friend. Leading? Can you guess? A two-month-old mule colt. Proud young animal, head high, glad to be at the picnic.

I wish you could have heard the presentation speech. I am certain that every town in every valley around heard the gales of laughter, shouts of excitement, celebrate, celebrate. Had any church ever before given its going away pastor a mule?

Some mules are extra-nice. This one was bred to his manners, plus love and games. He had a beautiful sorrel coat, long ears, laughing eyes. So with master leading, up came the two-month-old baby straight to the microphone where he gave a loud bray, surveyed the balloons, relished the children petting him, brayed again into the mike and off he went to meet the older folks. I had never seen anything like it. But then, I'd never known a congregation like this either.

The official name of our little church was Hawley Memorial Presbyterian, so what should we name the mule child? So let's have a contest, and guess who won? Martha won with "Hawley Moses."

Remember now, Hawley Moses was no donkey. His father was a giant mule jack named Floyd; his mother a two thousand pound Belgian mare. Belgian show horses and giant mules were Herb's specialty. True to Amish tradition, he farmed with horses and mules—big horses, big, big mules. So with his big mule daddy and big horse mamma, Moses was sure to grow big, and he did. Huge.

What would you do if someone gave you a mule which would grow not big but huge? That's what I wondered. Sure, I loved mules, but I'd never owned one. A small donkey I might manage, but this? You can tell the future size of a mule colt when he is two months old by measuring the distance from knee to hoof. That's the clue. By formula known to mule men, you can predict the size of your future mule—and Moses' measurement was ultra-generous.

We were moving to Athens, Georgia, to be near our youngest grandchildren. An exciting move to a three-acre site. No house yet, but big red barn. Stalls, haymow, the works. Wouldn't this be exactly the place for a big red mule? Yes, a perfect match, except for two things. First, we had a house to build, and until it was finished we'd be living away from the site. Second, I knew exactly zero about how to care for a mule. I did know he wouldn't be two months old and living with his mother forever. Someday he'd be four months, weaned, and then they would deliver him to me. In an elegant delivery van they would deliver him.

Whatever could I do? I could pray, and I did. Plenty. I also hung Moses' picture at a prominent spot in the workshop of my barn. (I pray better with pictures.)

Next, an almost unbelievable happening. To rebuild our barn and construct our new home we had hired a young contractor named Smith Wilson. Special name for a very special gentleman.

Are you ready for this? On that very day when I nailed Hawley Moses' picture to my shop wall, in came Smith. The minute he saw my mule picture, Smith stopped in his tracks, looked from picture to me, from me to picture.

Conversation:

"Where did you get that picture? Colt, isn't he? Don't think I've ever seen such a mule colt." What, where, who, etc.

"He's my colt. His name is Hawley Moses, and he's arriving here next week."

"No kidding!"

Then I told him the story. But before I closed my tale of fun and of woe, I said, "Smith, I don't know thing one about taking care of a mule, especially a mule colt. Do you know anyone in this area who could help me?"

"Dr. Shedd," he said, "Do you know I am president of the Georgia Draft Horse and Mule Association?"

Did I know? I didn't even know there *was* a Georgia Draft Horse and Mule Association.

Unbelievable. One preacher mule owner, about to be delivered one mammoth mule colt. One young contractor whose hobby is draft horses and mules. Here they are meeting in a rebuilt barn. Before them the picture of one baby mule. Giant baby mule. And for me one giant happening put together by... angels?

So he made me an offer, and I accepted. He would take Hawley Moses to his small farm down the road not far from us. He would love Moses through his colt days, train him to halter and harness, do all the things a mule needs done to make him one fine mule. And that's what he did.

So Moses grew and grew until he became gigantic, big, big fun. And all the veteran mule men who came to see him, all who saw him at the shows said in unison, "Seventeen and a half hands? Never saw anything like it."

Why did Moses grow so big? Was it because of that exciting party with the balloons and gales of laughter? Everyone knows that babies do better with a happy start and lots of love.

No author worth the name would need to labor the point of this story, would he? But I do have some questions you might like to muse through with me:

Is there a special department in heaven to answer this kind of prayer from a bewildered preacher, "Lord, Hawley Moses is coming soon. He is only four months old and you know that I don't know what I need to know about mules. Can you help me with this one?"

Did God know which contractor we would need for rebuilding our barn, constructing our home, *and helping with our mule?*

Could anyone who believes even a little have an experience like this and not believe in angels?

Never hesitate to ask the heavenly Father
for help with anything.
He cares about everyperson, every creature, everything.

Calico Hospice Lady

*M*anx cats are not your ordinary, pedestrian cats. In the official nomenclature we call them "Stumpies" (short tail) and "Rumpies" (no tail). The back legs of Manx cats make them high behind, and they are leapers to great heights. If there were derbies for cats, it would be no contest. Without a tail holding them back, Manx cats are very, very fast. When they turn it to high speed and hop like a kangaroo, they can outrun almost anything. But there are other differences more important.

The well-bred Manx has an altogether different philosophy from even its fancy cousins. Cat fanciers know that most cats will rub against whatever leg is available for one reason only. It makes the cat feel good! But Manx cats, somewhere in their evolving, turned a corner. From then on life for them was not first to be loved, but to love. Henceforth, they would rub against people's legs to make the *people* feel good!

And that brings us to Dinah. Early in our marriage Martha and I had raised Manx cats as a hobby. (That's how I know what I know about Manx cats.) So in our retirement, we decided to look for a Manx; a nice memento of the happy cat years. But no luck. No Manx.

Our next favorite cat being calico, we opted to settle for our second choice. We studied the classified ads, pet column, and one night there it was:

"Found. Calico kitten. Very gentle female. If she belongs to you, won't you please call 749-2738."

She wasn't ours—not then—but taking a chance, we dialed the number to leave our name. "In case the true owners don't surface, please put us on your interested list."

"What list?" they asked. "You're our first caller. Can't you come right away? We're allergic to cats. Please. We've run the ad for two weeks without one single inquiry. Please come and look at her. Please."

So I went, alone. Martha wasn't feeling well, which was very unusual. Looking back now, I know these must have been the first days of her last days.

When I arrived at their door, the whole family came to meet me: father, mother, daughter, son, two of them wheezing—and one small calico, purring.

But that's not all. *This was a calico Manx!* (A very rare combination, but she was typically Manx in every way, including one I forgot to mention: Manx are great greeters.)

They welcomed me in and immediately began to explain, "She doesn't have a tail, but we can almost guarantee you'll love her anyway."

And we did. Martha took to the little lady immediately, and the little lady to Martha. It was love at first sight both ways.

"Only you must understand, little lady," Martha said, "all cats in our family are outdoor cats." House rule, an established rule from day one with our first cat.

We named her Dinah. All our Manx cats had biblical names—Phinehas, Artaxerxes, Saul, Keturah, Dorcas, Mehetabel, and Mary (born Christmas day). And now, Dinah, from the story of Leah, who bore her husband son after son after son, up to six. And then came this tender addition: "Later she gave birth to a daughter and named her Dinah" (Genesis 30:21 NIV).

Dinah did not like the "No cats in the house" rule. For weeks she would slip in at every opportunity. She was a genius at hiding when we went to catch her. But since Martha couldn't abide cats in the house, I really worked at keeping her out. "Dinah, rules being what they are, you are turning into a real nuisance. Slip in, hide, be seized, out you go—this has to end. My energy level isn't up to it any longer, Dinah. Martha is sick, and my attention from this day on cannot be given to chasing cats. Please try to understand."

Do you believe cats can comprehend human emergencies? Is it possible for an animal to finally get a message which calls forth sympathy? It was with Dinah. I tell you true: from that day on it was almost pathetic. Days, weeks, the little calico cat sat outside our big den door. Looking in, she seemed to be asking, "Won't somebody come out to hold me, pet me, visit?"

Why had she stopped dashing for the interior whenever the door opened? Why was she waiting so patiently?

Then one night weeks later, Martha had a sinking spell, way down. This was the beginning of the scary times. Down, down to the brink, but once again she'd come back, and we would hope again. Sometimes we would be hopeful together. Sometimes when she'd go too far away, I would be hopeful alone.

It was one of those "so alone" days when Dinah broke the rule. When the den door opened, completely out of character for her these days, there she came. She made a mad dash through the door into Martha's room, up on Martha's bed. She settled down, way down, and began to purr.

Is there any sound more soothing than the rhythmic purring of a cat? Probably only one thing more soothing, and that is the purr of a loving cat, like Dinah.

I will never forget that moment, a moment of holy meaning. As I sat there beside them, slowly Martha came back, back to consciousness. She opened her eyes, looked around, saw who her visitor was, and said, "Kitty?!" Question mark! Exclamation point! Next she turned to me and smiled her "This is so fine" smile. Then she fell away again. From that point on Dinah stayed in Martha's bed or on her lap. Only now and then she took brief leave to come and check on me.

"Kinship with all life" is a provocative term. It is used frequently by experts who have majored in animal-human relationships. Did the Creator make all life with an interlocking support system? Do his concerns for all extend to every member of the family, including pets?

That smile Martha smiled when Dinah came to her bed said more to me than I have told you. "People in; cats out" was Martha's rule, not mine. Never a point of contention between us, simply an item understood. We saved our contention for bigger things (Well, mostly).

Yet when she smiled that particular moment out of her shadows, I knew the meaning of her smile. "Since we both believe in 'kinship with all life,' let her stay. I like her here."

In this revision of the rules, Dinah served. Day after day, night after night, week after week, there she was. Dear little calico hospice lady, there to purr, there to comfort, there to bless. Another brush of an angel's wing.

God and the Unhappy Surprises

*The most beautiful experience we can have
is the mysterious... the existence of some
things we cannot penetrate... which only in
their primitive forms are accessible to our
minds... It is this knowledge and this emotion
that constitute true religiosity. In this sense I
am a deeply religious man.*   Albert Einstein

Sometimes I am angry at God. Why would God send an angel to make me glad this time? But next time, no angel, no blessing, nothing but hurt and despair. Why? It doesn't make sense, Lord. If you really do have all those angels under your control, where were they when I needed them yesterday? Or last week? Or six years ago when my sky fell in? And sometimes even our Bible stories seem fuzzy with unknowns. Why?

"Why Does It Rain on My Uncle's Farm?"

*A*uthors receive letters from many readers. It's an interesting part of our lives, but sometimes the questions are almost too much. This one came from Shelly, a high-school sophomore in Nebraska. It gets dry in the Cornhusker state sometimes, and this has been one hard year. The farmers' corn has dried up and what will they feed the cattle?

She begins with a word of appreciation.

"I read your book *The Stork is Dead,* and it helped me. I noticed you are a minister so I am writing you about something that is bothering me. We are having a hard time on the farm this year because of no rain. My father is worried about paying the bills and the bank. All the farmers are worried.

"My folks are good people. We go to church, my mom and I sing in the choir, and my father is a deacon. My parents do so many good things. They grow more food than we need and give to poor people.

"I guess what bothers me most is *why does it rain on my uncle's farm?* He lives seventy miles away, and his crops are looking good. I probably shouldn't say this, but my uncle is mean. I don't see how my aunt stands him; he is so awful to her. He is awful to my cousins too, and nobody likes him. He swears a lot, and he doesn't go to church. I am not sure he even believes in God. So why does he get rain and we don't? Do you know what I'm asking? Do you think it's fair?..."

and her hurt goes on.

No, Shelly, I don't think it's fair. And yes, I do know what you're asking. Many times I've seen good things happen to bad people and it makes me wonder. I've also seen terrible things happen to good people, and if I were running the world, I'd make it rain on your farm.

The only word I can think of to describe all this is *mystery*. It's like a riddle nobody ever solved completely. And this kind of mystery goes way back, I suppose, to the beginning of time. It certainly goes back as far as the Old Testament book of Job.

Job is the story of a good man who lost his farms, his livestock, his money, his health and then the worst of all—he lost his family. But though he doubted sometimes and complained, he wouldn't give up his faith in God. And the story ends on this happy note: "The Lord blessed the latter part of Job's life more than the first" (Job 42:12).

That's what I believe happens to all of us when we refuse to give up our faith. It takes a strong faith to believe in God's eternal goodness when life is so hard. Sometimes we learn something valuable from the hard times while we are still living on earth. But sometimes we will not know the answer to our "Why?" questions until we get to heaven.

The Bible says, "He causes his sun to rise on the evil and on the good, and sends rain on the righteous and the unrighteous" (Matthew 5:45). Someday when we are in heaven, we can ask the Lord exactly why he does things the way he does things. And when we have heard his story, I think we'll say, "That's amazing Lord… I never would have thought of anything so wonderful."

"Why Would This Happen to My Study Bible?"

$\mathcal{T}$welve-by-twelve is not a large room, but it was exactly right for me. The officers of my church had built it in our back yard. They'd done it with their own hands, and it was tidy. Desk, file, bookshelves, and a reclining chair for resting. Built of cedar inside and out, this was my writing sanctuary. Comfort in the summer, comfort in the winter, they'd thought of that, too. High up toward the ceiling was an effective air conditioner-heating unit.

They'd done all this because they were worried about their young pastor. The church was growing so fast. In addition to preaching, he was writing. Wouldn't it be nice if he had a place of retreat? A hideaway with no phone? Plus time, approved by the officers, for uninterrupted writing?

Concern. That's a caring word from church leaders for their minister. But they'd never thought of the forthcoming disaster, and neither had I.

Many serious Christians have their personal study Bible with note after note written directly on page after page. Slips of paper at special passages. All kinds of attention-getters, some with pencil, others with colored marker, red, yellow, blue, green.

Supposing your personal study Bible should be destroyed? That would be a disaster, wouldn't it? It would, and I know because that's what happened to my study Bible in my twelve-by-twelve hideaway.

As everyone knows, air conditioners are built to empty their water outside. But without warning the conditioner in my writing hideaway went awry. Without warning something blocked its normal flow, and there came what must have been torrents of water. Pouring down the wall, flooding the floor, and woe of woes for me—soaking my study Bible, too.

Obviously I should not have had such a precious book on that table below the air conditioner. But I had chosen this spot for a good reason. I like to leave my study Bible open where I can see its colorful underlinings. I also like to glance at the question marks, exclamation points, the notes on this and that.

We've all had our own catastrophic moments, when something precious goes out of our lives forever. One day, one hour, one dreadful moment. And this was one of my most dreadful ever. That day when I opened the door, there was my study Bible floating in a pool of water.

Red, yellow, blue, green markings and black print flooded off the pages to mix with the colors. Pages so wet they could never be separated. How long had all this taken? No one will ever know. I'd been gone three days.

Experts tell us that a period of mourning is important after significant losses. But they also tell us that these should not go on too long. I mourned, and it went on too long. But didn't I deserve some extended time to sulk and cry and ask God, "Why?" After all, here in my devastated Bible were four years of class notes from college. All the wisdom of my wonderful tutor (the one who liked to talk angels with me), his thoughts wiped out permanently too. My Bible notes from seminary lectures.

"Who hath woe? Who hath sorrow?... Who hath redness of eyes?" The Bible says (Proverbs 23:29-30) it's he who tarries too long at the wine. But I can attest to this: He also hath woe who tarries too long before his favorite Bible flooded away.

Then one day I felt that inner nudge again. A new spirit. A new idea, almost like a voice, from way down at the center.

"Why not buy another Bible, Charlie, to take the place of your ruined favorite? Salvage what you can from the flooded ruin. Then day after day, month after month, go back over the terrain you've traveled. Make new notes, color again with red, yellow, blue, green. This way, won't you some day know your Bible twice as well as you know it now?"

Were there angels at work anywhere in this saga of my water-flooded Bible? I don't know. But I do know this. Looking back on seventy-eight years, some of the hardest things that ever happened to me had a blessing in them somewhere.

Do you suppose there might be a special group of angels assigned to scatter seeds in our hopelessness? I think there must be.

So often in the dark moments—little, big, or catastrophic—you may have sensed it, too. Hidden in the heavy happening is the brush of an angel's wing come to comfort and encourage; come to show us how we can make something good out of the bad; come to turn the devastation into an eventual victory.

"Why Should I Lose My Voice?"

There are many nice things about aging. Mature now, you can scan your days gone by and see the pattern. Ups, downs, ins, outs, and roundabouts leading somewhere. Sure, there'll be some negative recall. But, if you're a Christian believer, you'll know where to go and what to do with the melancholy. Then, having "sought the Lord" with that, you can look out across the terrain of yesterday and smile. You can laugh, too, and cry a little and "praise God from whom all blessings flow."

There was one dramatic happening in my life which I thought for sure would finish me. Measured any way, the news was a bummer. One young minister had a tumor on his larynx, and I was the minister.

The doctors said, "We can remove it, and we should.

But even if it isn't malignant, going into the larynx could damage your vocal cords. This might silence your career as a preacher."

What can a preacher do without his voice? One possibility for me was a carpenter's shop. In high school, my favorite class was woodworking. My manual training teacher would put his arm around me and say, "Charlie, God has given you a special reverence for wood." I liked that: "reverence for wood." And he was right. I loved working with wood and tools, fitting this to that, creating items of my own design.

Or maybe I could be a farmer. Crops and animals, these were for me too. But back in the big depression years, who had the money to begin farming? In debt for seven years of schooling, I certainly didn't. Then there was pumping gas, clerking in a store, delivering mail. But didn't these all require a voice?

With the solution pending, we drove to Omaha for the operation. I can still remember the verse we turned to that morning on our way to the hospital. Psalm 34:4, "I sought the Lord, and he heard me, and delivered me from all my fears." Wonderful verse, except it didn't work that way for me. Here was stubborn Charlie, still hanging on to the "awful-awfuls."

Yet the post-operation news was good. And are there any more beautiful words in the English language than: "*It is not malignant*"? "However," the surgeon said, "We had to go deep. The prognosis still holds. With your larynx so weakened, you might lose your voice." I didn't. Except temporarily. In the years to follow I did have days and weeks when I could barely make a sound. For six weeks, two or three months, absolute silence. As I looked to the future with no voice and no permanent income, this was a troubling time.

Since I needed to spare my vocal chords, I spent many hours in my workshop. Building, planning, considering furniture designs which might be marketable. I worked long at my bench. And it was one great day for me when I sold the plans for one of my projects to *Popular Mechanics*. Big deal. Big profit.

More articles with designs from my shop followed in the writing markets. Then one day a light came on. Why couldn't I be writing other things? So off I went to the magazine stand. Mrs. Fowler ran the news shop and we had been friends for some time. God bless her fertile imagination. Mrs. Fowler would say, "I'd love to help you become a magazine writer, Charlie. So you sit here on my floor. Study what the publishers are buying. Go ahead, take notes, get addresses, write down the names of editors. Then send a query letter and ask if they'd be interested in the things you'd like to write."

Thank you, Mrs. Fowler. I did what you suggested. From your place in heaven you'll remember the record. Fifty-five magazine articles I sold in those early years. What if they did average eleven rejections each? So? Doesn't the Bible say, "In due season we shall reap, *if we faint not*" (Galatians 6:9 KJV)?

Next came books—two of which became immediate

best-sellers. Meaning dollars to underwrite a tricky throat. But dollars, too, for sharing. The Christian believes that God has a plan for underwriting his Kingdom. And believing that, we were able to open a foundation. A foundation dedicated to agricultural missions, the purchase of animals, and hunger relief.

Around the world our dollars went. From project to project in many lands: chickens and rabbits, water buffalo and pigs, Belgian horses and mules, sheep and goats; to the Philippines, to Thailand and Korea, to Zaire and Nigeria, to India and Haiti. And in our own country cattle, riding horses, pigs, bees, and fish to a farm for retarded children in Virginia.

Something to be proud of? No. Something to praise the Lord for? Yes!

Thank you, heavenly Father, for the way you can turn a tumor on the larynx into a writing career. Thank you for the way you can take a writing career and turn that into missions. Inscribe it on my heart and keep me believing it deep inside...

Beauty for ashes,
the oil of joy for mourning
the garment of praise for the spirit of heaviness.
Isaiah 61:30

"Why Would You Let Me Be So Embarrassed?"

*C*ertain happenings which we think are so hard at the time seem minor looking back. One day we might even smile and say, "Some of my major embarrassments were really not all that bad."

At seventy-eight, that's how I feel about my career as a high-school wrestler.

Fact: In an Iowa YMCA tournament, now more than sixty years ago, I set a state record! I set the record for being thrown quicker than anyone ever in the state finals. Flat on my back, subdued in TWELVE seconds!

Through the years I've rewrestled that state championship meet over and over. There he stands, Tub Wright, my adversary. Hands held high, on his way to full scholarship at a Big Ten university. And there am I flat on my back, mortified.

If you are an Iowa wrestling fan, you'll know the truth of this statement: Even to reach the state finals was and is impressive. Today, Iowa University wins the national championship regularly. Back when I was wrestling, Iowa State would win it sometimes, too.

My high school did not offer wrestling, so I trained at the "Y" in a neighboring city. Long bus rides, long lessons from the coach, long workouts. It's been a long, long time since my big put-down, yet I can still remember the moment as though it were twelve seconds ago.

"Tub" was a huge farm boy from southern Iowa, and very likeable. We worked together the next summer at a "Y" camp. For evening entertainment we would suit up and put on the *Tub and Charlie* show. Great fun for the evening crowds full of Iowa wrestling fans. I liked it. Especially I liked this. Sometimes Tub would win, some-times I would. That restored my ego a bit. But forever the dominant memory. I lost the state championship.

Yet other memories travel quickly, too (as in twelve seconds) to bring more permanent lessons.

What character forming valuables did I garner from that single put-down?

- A genuine sympathy for losers and the laughed-at.
- A sense of respect for those who are a little bit (or face it Charlie) much, much better.
- A definite understanding that I will not always win and neither do I need to.

Congratulations Tub. You were the state champion that year, and I salute you. But looking back I see this plainly now—because he loves us, the Lord can take even a high-school wrestler's humiliation and weave some character from it.

When Jesus Asked "Why?"

"Where were you, Father, when I prayed from the midst of my pain and no answer came? Nothing but stony silence. Zero help. Zero help from earth or heaven or anywhere. No miracle this time. Only agony, tears, and utter darkness of soul. Blackness by day, and blacker still the darkness of night. Questions screaming, moaning. Where are you, Father? Where have you been with your deliverance?"

> *"My God, my God, why hast thou forsaken me?"*
> **Matthew 27:46 KJV**

You've felt the spikes of rejection, haven't you? The thorns of loss, the cross of total despair. From the darkness of your tomb, you've questioned the God who would allow such suffering.

But praise his holy name. Deep in our soul haven't we also heard the Resurrection angel with his announcement just for us: "He is not here for He is risen!" (Matthew 28:6 KJV).

TWELVE

Staying in Shape for the Angels
— Part One —

There is a secret
to staying in shape for the angels.

And for me this secret of secrets
can best be summed up
in these three words:

THE INDWELLING CHRIST

An Evening Meal with My Lord

One of my all-time favorite Bible verses is Revelation 3:20—"Behold, I stand at the door, and knock: If any man hear my voice, and open the door, I will come in to him and will sup with him." (KJV)

It sounds so simple, doesn't it? "Sup" in biblical language usually means the evening meal. We invite him for supper.

Such a charming guest. After the blessing, he begins asking us about us. Courtesy plus. Manners at their best. But now, with supper ended, where have all the manners gone?

He stands and says, "Let's have a look around." Then he leads the way, but have you ever had a guest like this? He lifts the rug. Dust. This week's dust. Last week's? Last month's?

Next, without even asking, he makes his way to the bedroom. Oh, no. He opens the drawers, looks in the closet and under the mattress. Embarrassing. And didn't we invite him only for *supper*?

Then, we can hardly believe this next move. To the attic. Attics fascinate him, he says. Old trunks, love letters, tax papers, magazines. All kinds of old things we'd been saving for no one's eyes but our own.

"Now to the basement, folks. Nothing like a basement. Especially the storeroom." So here we are in the storeroom. Boxes with their labels: General Memories, Precious Memories, Memories We Should Have Let Go. Isn't this getting too personal? Meddling?

"Come, Lord. Time for dessert."

"Thank you. Not tonight."

Then suddenly he is gone.

"Gone?" Gone permanently? No, gone to give us time for thinking it through. Thinking what through? Thinking through the full scope of his statement: "I stand at *every single door* and knock. Conscious, Subconscious, Ego, Superego, Id. Every part. No exceptions. No excuses.

Ours is the one hundred percent Lord. And this is his one hundred percent claimer.

I want one hundred percent access
to one hundred percent of you.

What's in It for Me?

"*B*ut if I give the Lord everything I have, what's left for me?"

It's a blunt question, heard often when we talk of Christian commitment. Usually it's couched in softer terms, but the underlying meaning is always there somewhere. And why not? Invite Christ into *every* room? Watch him rearrange the furniture? Have things *his* way? And finally, because he insists, we must give him title to the place. Our soul is no longer ours. It's his.

So this is the Christian life? I give him my all? All? So what do I get? What's in it for me?

Here is one answer. The Bible's most complete answer: Galatians 5:22-23, "The fruit of the Spirit is love, joy, peace, longsuffering, gentleness, goodness, faith, meekness, temperance..." (KJV).

Researching the interpretations of other translators, we find some additional attributes worth pondering. From various versions, the scholars tell us what the original wording means to them.

Kindness

Patience

Fidelity

Forbearance

Self-restraint

Self-control

Faithfulness

Generosity

Trustfulness

Humility

Straight from The Book, these are the answers to our question, "What's in It for Me?"

Yet isn't there another answer? A beautiful answer. Exciting.

Since angels exist to represent God and serve him, with the Indwelling Christ really indwelling us, there are sure to be more angels coming our way.

Return of the Pipes

He wants it all?
He wouldn't be asking us to give
up even our comfortable little
habits, would he?
Or would he?

*I*f ever your travels find you along the East Coast,
here's an unusual stop you certainly will enjoy. As
you see the signs for Jekyll Island, Georgia, you're near-
ing Florida. Several miles out in the Atlantic, you'll find a
fascinating interlude in your schedule. This is a state
park, groomed to the utmost. Here you will view the
restored "Old Millionaires' Hotel and Cottages." What
would it be like to live in such opulence?

Jekyll Island boasts magnificent golf courses, bicycle
trails and leisurely roads. Deer and wildlife roam free.
Nine miles of white beach invite visitors to take a walk,
shells underfoot, pelicans overhead. Driftwood and turtles
along the shore. You can sit for a spell facing the ocean,
where you can see forever.

But one of the most fascinating attractions on Jekyll Island is the "Faces of Christ" room at the Jekyll Community Presbyterian Church.

Do you ever wonder, "What did Jesus *really* look like?" We know that nobody knows for sure. Yet you'll enjoy the possibilities if you sit in this quiet room and ponder the faces.

Here is the laughing Christ and one who looks like a Notre Dame fullback. The one over here in overalls and that one in a business suit. A black Jesus, an Indian Jesus, an Asian Jesus, all there for your musing. Drawings and paintings, sculpted stone and metal, carvings from wood … they'll stretch your mind and your soul.

I know what that collection can do to the human heart because I collected it. I was a young pastor in Houston, Texas, organizing a new congregation which was growing like crazy. We happened to be located at one of the most strategic corners in our city. But that was only one reason why we grew.

Two basic commitments marked this church "Different." First, everyone in our membership was prayed for every day by someone. Which also meant, the way it was done, that every member was praying for some other member. By name. Every day. Everyone, no exception, prayed for and praying.

Commitment two was a daring "Dollar for Dollar" mission program. "Impossible," they said, "Insane. Crazy." Others, in even more graphic terms called it "Bankruptcy for Jesus."

Yet that's what this new congregation voted, and that's

exactly what they did. Unrealistic as it sounded, this was the pledge:

"Every dollar spent for our own needs will be matched with another dollar for Kingdom needs beyond our local congregation."

And the people came. From all over the city they came to join these courageous souls who were praying and giving like nothing they'd ever experienced before. So they prayed and they gave and they flourished.

Then I began asking myself: How can I ever grow spiritually strong enough to pastor a church like this? Though I was having the time of my life in some ways, in others *I was not what I knew I should be.*

I did not know my Lord personally. Of course I knew Christ as the perfect revelation of God. I also knew him as the perfect revelation of what I ought to be, and that made me nervous. I was sure he wanted us to be better friends.

So I decided I must get down to business. I prayed my "Get-down-to-business" prayer, the hardest prayer I ever pray:

"Lord, show me what to do, and I will do it."

That is one tough prayer. It's easy to pray it only part way. "Lord, what I really mean is, show me what to do so I can decide if I really want to do it."

But this time I did mean "Show me, and *I will do what you show me."* What he showed me was a great idea.

I was cruising the picture department of a Christian bookstore. I have always especially liked pictures of interesting faces. Drawings, paintings, masterpieces, calendars, watercolors, pastels and oils; any interesting face, I'll like it. There among the faces of Jesus was one I'd never seen before, and I liked it. Picking it up, I stroked the frame and pondered. Then when I put it down, "the hand thing" happened again. I call it "the hand thing" because it has happened to me so much I know this might be a signal. For a moment, sometimes a few fleeting seconds, sometimes minutes, my hand seems to hesitate. *Wait.* So I wait. I leave my hand where it is and listen. Sometimes from deep inside me I hear a whisper. Is this the voice of the Lord? An angel? This time with my hand on the picture, I heard:

Charlie, why not start a collection, "The Faces of Jesus," right now, beginning with this one?

That next Sunday I told my congregation what I was planning, and I invited them to participate. "If you have a favorite face of Jesus you can loan us temporarily, bring it in. We'll hang them all and enjoy them together."

My study was a large room with plenty of wall space for plenty of pictures. So they brought theirs and I hung mine. Then, because so many contributed, we organized a Faces of Jesus Picture Committee. Every three months they would rearrange, hang the new, return the loaners, plan special showings.

You've already guessed what was happening to me.

Each day as I looked up I would see those faces of Jesus looking at me. Then gradually each picture seemed to take on its own particular character trait. Honesty. Tenderness. Courage. Good cheer. Love. Patience. Mercy. *Sacrifice. Commitment. Renunciation.* These last three finally did my pipes in.

One of my favorite diversions during those days was smoking a pipe. I actually don't remember how I got into this, but somehow tobacco pipes had always fascinated me. It may have happened back there in my courting days when I loved to watch my Danish father-in-law with his pipe. In near reverence he would clean his pipe, fill it, draw on it, and blow smoke rings to absolute perfection.

I had created a habit I thoroughly enjoyed. And the pipe smokers in my congregation kept me well-supplied with new pipes, plus their favorite tobacco.

One day as I was studying my faces of Jesus pictures, it happened. I heard that voice from the inner chamber again.

"In which of these faces would a pipe look good?"

From that moment I seemed to know my pipes had to go.

But not right away.

For several summers we'd been spending our vacation at Playmore Beach, Rocky Mount, a quiet little resort for families on the Lake of the Ozarks. Protected cove, big docks, ideal swimming. Now there we were again and, as usual, I'd brought my pipes along. I told the Lord, "I really have quit, you know. But this is vacation, isn't it? Far from the Faces of Jesus collection, far from the youth groups and all those I might influence. What's wrong with a dreamy pipeful up here?"

I got out my pipe box and handled my pipes one by one. But "handle" reminded me of "hand." And "hand" reminded me of "the hand of the Lord." And "the hand of the Lord" reminded me of the whispers. And "the whisper" said *"Hand them over!"*

You know what happened. The Lord and I had it out. Once and for all we settled it. His way.

On the appointed morning I took up my pipe box. My beloved pipe box with all those wonderful pipes in hand, and I rowed out to the middle of the lake. At least a half mile from our cabin, I lifted the box gently and dropped it over the side of the boat. "Good-bye, you poor dears. This I am doing for the Lord, and this is farewell forever. May you rest in peace."

Only they didn't.

The next morning where do you suppose my pipes were? *They had washed up on our very beach, right there in front of our cabin!*

One hundred cabins where they could have settled.

Or was it two hundred? One half mile they'd traveled. Or was it several miles bouncing on the lake before they decided to come home?

You can imagine the long talks we had that day, Martha and I. She knew I loved my pipes and how much I wanted to keep them. She liked them, too. They made her think of her father. Now, I argued again. Couldn't I keep them at least as souvenirs of an unbelievable happening? Might I have possibly made the wrong decision? Had I been unduly pious about my faces of Jesus?

Over and over I argued, but always back to the same cruel words—Renunciation. Surrender. Commitment.

The next morning, while it was barely day, I rowed back to the middle of the lake. Martha with me this time, to hold my hand. With the other hand, one by one I took each pipe, dropped that particular old friend overboard, and watched it sink to the bottom of the lake. *"There you are, Lord. This time they're yours."*

The faces of Christ had done their work.

Today, the "Faces of Jesus" collection is in a special room built for it at the lovely Jekyll Community Presbyterian Church.

If you're ever in the area, do drop by and see it. Only here's a warning for you. If you get the full message of all those faces, you might never be the same again.

Forever, this is his call to us:

All I want is all of you for all of Me.

"God has celestial vacuum cleaners which His angels can use to draw out all poisons, toxins, and infections in our souls and bodies. So let us invite the Lord to send a corps of angel cleaners, and put them to work right now. As they are invisible, they can penetrate into any pocket or hidden area in our lives, and turn on their celestial vacuums." **Glenn Clark**

Staying in Shape for the Angels
— Part Two —

When Peter began swinging his sword to settle things,
Jesus stopped him, "If I needed your kind of help,
I could call for twelve legions of angels,
and they would be here immediately."

That is the kind of Lord
who wants to live in us,
but he insists on living his way in our hearts.

The Majors

Some of my friends still tell me that life with the Inner Christ is simple. Invite him in, give him the keys, and he takes it from there. Easy does it.

It is not that way with me. Any time I want the keys back, he hands them over. He's gone, and the place is mine again. So what can I do to make this commitment stick?

For me there are three major helps to consistency. They are not presented here in the order of their importance. Instead I see them as part of a whole, and we'll begin with The Book.

MAJOR ONE—THE BOOK

The more I am faithful to my Bible study, the more I feel God entering my soul to work in me and through me. And I am that much more alert to the brush of an angel's wing—an angel come to bless and use me.

Reading, studying, thinking. From Genesis to Revelation, I make my pilgrimage through Old Testament and New. As I travel these roads, I learn God's way of doing things. I see what he has accomplished with others. But even more, I also understand clearly what he can do with ordinary folks like me. I learn, too, how he wants me to cooperate.

I am grateful to the Bible scholars for all they've taught me. But to a mind like mine, God speaks in language clear and everyday. In one verse, one chapter, or even a single word, he teaches me.

So this I have learned. The more I am faithful to my own personally designed method of Bible study, the better it goes. Why? Because as I study, God indwells my soul and brings his angels with him.

Psalm 119:11 is a great "how to" statement for angel believers. "Thy word have I hid in my heart." Have I?

MAJOR TWO—PRAYER

The more I pray, the more I understand the Lord and how he does things.

Prayer is conversation with the Lord. Prayer is dialogue. Prayer is sharing. It's my talk and his talk. For that deeper life with God, I must have times of inner stillness, aligning my direction with his.

Ours is one hurry, hurry world, isn't it? Zip, zam, and zowie—we measure success by how much and how many. But this harassed and harried frenzy is not new.

Pressure was a constant threat for the Master, too. Hustle and bustle. Five times the Gospels tell us Jesus could not accomplish what he hoped to get done "for the press." The "press" as in urgency. "Press" as in pressure from outside and in. Has a familiar ring, doesn't it?

Such a large crowd gathered that Jesus and his disciples had no time to eat. Mark 3:20 TEV

So how did Christ manage the press, the crowds? He went off by himself—to the mountain, to the garden, to the upper room, to the lower deck.

Why?

For time alone with the Father.

Of course we can know our Lord in the marketplace. If we ask him, he will be with us in our busyness. But for many, this is true: We can sense God best in the push and shove when we have taken time to be with him alone.

Go away by yourself, all alone, and shut the door behind you and pray. Matthew 6:6

What is the greatest day in anyone's prayer life? I think it is when we shift our emphasis from "me" to "Thee." Now instead of first asking God to answer our prayers, we pray: "Lord, I want to answer your original prayer for me on the day of my creation. And may I learn to help others answer your prayers for them too."

MAJOR THREE—LOVE

The more I love and work at loving, the more I hear God's whispers.

Too often it requires serious discipline for me to love as Jesus loved. As I watch, I see him focusing on each individual. I need that. One of the hardest disciplines for some of us is concentration on *one person at a time.* Yet when we look at Christ's attitudes toward people, we see him loving the variant segments of humankind. Races, classes, types, strata of society, and individuals. He loved them all. No, he didn't *like* them all, and he doesn't call us to do that either.

But *love?* Yes. For heaven's sake, Lord, help me to love as you loved the individual, the group, the world.

Jesus says, "This is my commandment, that you love one another, as I have loved you" (John 15:12).

These I must keep before me as the three major factors to Christian commitment: Bible study, prayer, and love. And most of my friends would say, "Me too!" Without them, we will not know the indwelling of Christ, the power of God, or the brush of an angel's wing. With them, we can know all three.

Go Where the Love Is Most Needed

*B*efore we go on to what I call "My Questions at the Mirror" I want to share with you one of the most beautiful witnesses I ever heard to the limitless love of God.

She was an old grandma, ninety-plus, and in the condition we'd all like to be in at ninety. She was seated next to me on a flight to Florida. A great-grandson was playing professional baseball that year, and he had sent her the plane fare to see him play. Next year he hoped to be in the majors. She was sure he'd make it, too. "Such a fine boy," she said. "One of my fifty-six 'Greats.'" The way she said it, I knew she wanted me to ask some questions. So I did.

"And how many children did it take you to get that many?"

"Thirteen. Then twenty-seven 'Grands' and fifty-six 'Greats.'"

"Say that again. How many altogether?"

"Ninety-six," she answered beaming. "And since you're interested, I can call them all by name. Would you like to hear?"

I would, and she did. Thirteen. Twenty-seven. Fifty-six. Lovingly she named them all.

"In order?" I asked.

"Yes," she said, "in order."

"How could you ever do that? Christmas and birthdays, special times and all the things a grandmother needs to remember. You must have some secret, don't you?"

"Oh, I do," she answered in her laughing voice. "I learned it when my own were little. When their daddy left, I was all they had. So with my thirteen, I asked the Lord each day to help me love each one with one hundred percent of my love. But that's not all. Each day I studied them till noon. Then when I could see which one needed two hundred percent, I gave that one two hundred percent. That's how I did it then, and that's the way I do it still with might near one hundred together in my heart. I pray for each one each day. Sometimes people tell me, 'You can't love more than one hundred percent at one time.' Now that's not true, is it? What they don't know is that when you ask the Lord for help, he just gives you more and more percents. After all, you know it's true—God has all the percents there is."

So true, Grandma. I needed your reminder. I hurry and worry. I fidget and fuss. I try to do too much too well, and all because too many of my inner doors are closed to the knocking of my Lord. From this day on, I will frame you, Grandma, in my soul. And every time I see you there, I will remember your message. God *does* have all the percents there is.

This is a beautiful witness to the limitless love of God.
The kind of love God wants us to have
The kind of love that gives God the opportunity
to love through us.
The kind of love that opens the way
for another brush of an angel's wing.

Personal Questions at the Mirror

"Soul, thou ailest here and here."
Saint Augustine

The great saints of history seem to share this one trait: they were experts at self-examination.

Certainly we can over-study what's going on inside. But can that ever be true, if we are checking for the right reason? And isn't this always the right reason: to measure ourselves by the life and spirit of our Lord.

So here are some of Charlie's questions to Charlie. These I share with you not that you might make them yours. You will do better with your own questions. Mine are for me. They reveal the roads of my soul in need of continual check-up and repair.

Some selections from my list:

I. *Have I been facing the total me in self-analysis?*

Looking back on my own unusual happenings, I see this clearly: the Lord does not wait for me to achieve true holiness before he uses me. Sometimes the angels come when I'm confessing my faults, facing some old ugly, mining the tunnels of yesterday, determining to do better. His angels seem to like these times. Repentence is step one on the road back home.

One sure law of the soul: the more I empty myself of the negative me, the more he can fill me with his positive presence.

II. *Am I constantly honing my intellect, sharpening the mind God gave me?*

An inquisitive mind has to be one of the Lord's rare gifts. Am I reading enough for the Divine mind to think new thoughts through me? Bible study, yes, but spiritual classics and devotional writing, too? All these I need in my personal library.

Yet that's not all. Am I reading enough for diversion, fun, plain entertainment? Do I sharpen my mind by hearing good speakers, attending lectures, seminars, workshops, joining a group? Will I listen to new ideas and expose myself to differing opinions?

"Lord, help me to be ever alert to quickening my mind for you."

III. *Am I taking good care of my body? Eating right? Sleeping right? Exercising? Staying in good physical condition?*

I might have been a better football player had I not been naturally lazy. And here I am at seventy-eight, still trying not to be lazy. I *know* all the good things I should be doing. Aerobics, weight lifting, walking, tennis. "Get ye up, ye couch potato." So I pray, "Lord help me to cherish this healthy body you've given me." And when I follow that prayer with action, my spiritual sensitivity seems heightened.

It is a good verse for the bulletin board of my soul:

> "Do you not know that your body is a temple of the Holy Spirit?" **1 Corinthians 6:19 NIV**

IV. *Am I ministering in the Lord's name to those who need the touch of his hand from my hand? More and more, am I becoming the kind of missionary an angel might use for blessing someone in need?*

Shouldn't "Mission" be the Christian's middle name? Selfishness is the antithesis of life with the Lord. For the sake of Christ, I need to be constantly checking my "otherness" quotient.

V. *Does the triumphal entry of Christ into my life include his triumphal entry into my pocketbook?*

Hard fact: I live in a world of great need. Every dollar, every cent I have is a gift from the Divine Hand. But is this a gift for me to keep or to share? Biblically, there is only one answer—the Lord does not need me as a bank. He wants me as a flowing place for his blessing to others.

VI. *Am I spending adequate time at home?*

The Son of Man had nowhere to lay his head. But I do. Is there a lonesome wife at my house? A husband looking for love? Are we making time for coalescing? Are my children getting from me all the parenting they need? It's a fact: loving well at my own address makes for better loving out there in the world.

VII. *Is there enough music in my life these days?*

Solo and chorus, praise and lament, trumpet and harp, timbrel and drum, they're all in The Book. The Bible's range of purpose and place for music is almost inexhaustible. But so is mine. The great works of the great artists; the twanging ballads of country and western; hymns and children's songs; all these I like, accompanied by big brass bands, piano, guitar, tambourine, accordian, xylophone, musical saw. You name it, I like it. I even like to sing alone in my shop. (My family also prefers that I sing alone in my shop.) But no matter the kind of music, this I do know: with the help of music, I stay tuned to the music in my soul.

"Thank you, Lord, for putting so much music inside me. Help me keep it all tuned upward."

VIII. *Am I developing my love for nature?*

Jesus was a nature lover. Sea and sky, flowers and trees, rivers and lakes, clouds and wind, birds and foxes, mountains and hills. All these Jesus learned from, taught from. Does my thrilling to all God's wonders open the way for him to do more of his wonders in me and through me?

IX. *Am I taking enough time for my hobbies?*

I love animals: horses, mules, ponies, rabbits, dogs, chickens. I've owned and bred them all. And here is a fascinating fact: so many of my extraordinary happenings have been associated with animals. What does all this say? I think it may be saying, "God uses our special interests to work through us."

Then to my favorite hobby: woodworking. When I get to heaven, won't there be training sessions for those of us who love wood? Imagine, learning straight from the Master Carpenter. With all kinds of time to learn from him, we'll shape, build, finish to perfection. This really will be heaven for me.

X. *Do I set aside time for doing nothing at all?*

"Don't just sit there. Do something."
"Idle hands are the devil's tools."
"Get a move on."

These are words I was raised on. But what about this advice from both Old Testament and New:
"Be still and know."
"Study to be quiet."
"He leadeth me beside still waters."
These also I need often and much.

"Lord, teach me the art of holy repose."

"Time you enjoy wasting is not wasted time." Maslow

Ten—that's enough that you might see what I mean by "Personal Questions at the Mirror." You've already sensed that this is not a six week's program for spiritual betterment.

Yet this I have learned, and you will too:

The more we work toward being
what the Lord intended,
that much more he makes it possible
for us to be what he intended.
And this too is true:
the more we work at becoming what he intended,
that much more the angels come to help us
be what he intended.

A Touch of Tomorrow's Wonder

"This is the Lord's doing;
it is marvelous in our eyes."
Psalm 118:23

The Tin Can Phone

*I*f you'd had a longtime interest in angels, these would be days to excite you. All around us, there is a growing curiosity about extraordinary happenings. Magazine articles, newspaper stories, plays and musicals, everywhere we see it's a fact. Suddenly angels, miracles, and things unexplainable come center stage.

What does all this mean, this fresh interest in angels? Is it only one more twitch of a jaded world looking for excitement? Or is it an indicator that ours is an age lonesome for assurance?

Whatever else it is, I see it as a sign of hope. Since I was thirteen—ever since my rescue from drowning in the water pipe—I have believed this wonderful promise of Scripture: "The earth shall be full of the knowledge of the Lord as the waters cover the sea" (Isaiah 11:9).

No human mind could possibly grasp all that means. But I did see something the other day that gave me a touch of tomorrow's wonders.

I was watching two of my neighbor children playing "Tin Can Phone." Each of them had a tin can, and a long string was drawn tight between them. Sister was on the porch, brother behind a tree. Out there in the yard, he pulled the string to its maximum, and they began talking. First shouting, then normal voice, then down to a whisper.

They're good friends of mine, and they saw me watching. "You really can hear," they shouted, and I knew they *were* hearing. I knew because of my own history. When we were children, my sister and I played "Tin Can Phone."

I asked one of my scientific friends to explain it. He said, "Tin actually does resonate, and almost anything drawn tight enough may carry reverberations."

As I mused on the children's game and my friend's observation, this thought kept coming back: "Do I really *need* to know the 'how' of God's amazing network? Perhaps for minds like mine, it is enough to be awed and grateful."

The Psalmist wrote, "Such knowledge is too wonderful for me" (Psalm 139:6).

It is, isn't it? Too wonderful for you and me together. Too wonderful to comprehend with the range of the human mind as it is today.

So when will we know all we'd like to know about the miracles and wonders of God? Some of you who are younger will know much more about "things too wonderful" as you grow older. But for those of us who believe the promises of The Book, there is another answer.

When we get to heaven, we'll know. There we will

have ears to hear clearly, minds to understand fully, new hearts to comprehend wholly.

And in this total comprehension, I think we'll see another thing. We will see that

All of us on earth are not first bodies with souls.
First, we are souls with bodies.

Small wonder we become confused trying to produce miracles on our own. We forget that we are born to be cooperators with God, working on his plan, his wonders.

I thrill to the marvels of our day's technology. But how about *this* for something to stretch our minds?

All of our own day's scientific advances in every field, all the new revelations in understanding humankind, all the new thrillers in communication, things which we have seen in our day, and those which our children and grandchildren will see... when compared to our Creator's original plan, all these together will seem like a brother and sister playing with a simple string drawn tight between their tin can phones.

We speak the wisdom of God in a mystery, even the hidden wisdom, which God ordained.... But as it is written, "Eye hath not seen, nor ear heard, neither have entered into the heart of man, the things which God hath prepared for them that love Him."

1 Corinthians 2:7–9 KJV

Invitation

*F*rom the author to the reader—

In your memory do you have an extraordinary happening or some mysterious brush of an angel's wing?

Tell me about it.
Let's do a book on:
More Brushes of an Angel's Wing

I'd like to hear from you. Send your stories to:

Dr. Charlie Shedd
Servant Publications
P.O. Box 8617
Ann Arbor, Michigan 48107

Other Books By Charlie Shedd

On Marriage

Letters To Karen
Letters To Philip
Talk To Me
Celebration in the Bedroom
How To Stay In Love
Bible Study Together: Making Marriage Last
  (Originally: Bible Study in Duet)
Praying Together: Making Marriage Last
  (Originally: Praying in Duet)

Ideas for Churches

The Exciting Church: Where People Really Pray
The Exciting Church: Where They Give Their Money
  Away
The Exciting Church: Where They Really Use the Bible
The Pastoral Ministry of Church Officers
How To Develop a Tithing Church
How To Develop a Praying Church

For Young People

The Stork Is Dead

You Are Somebody Special
How To Know If You're Really In Love

Biography

Remember, I Love You: Martha's Story

For Parents and Grandparents

You Can Be A Great Parent
   (Originally: Promises To Peter)
Smart Dads I Know
The Best Dad Is A Good Lover
A Dad Is For Spending Time With
Is Your Family Turned On?
Grandparents: Then God Created Grandparents
Grandparents: Family Book
Tell Me A Story: Stories for Grandchildren

For Help on Managing Your Life

Time For All Things
The Fat Is In Your Head
Devotions For Dieters
Pray Your Weight Away
Getting Through To The Wonderful You
Word Focusing: A New Way To Pray

On Writing

If I Can Write, You Can Write

To contact Charlie Shedd
for speaking engagements,
write or call

Michael McKinney
McKinney Associates, Inc.
P.O. Box 5162
Louisville, KY 40205
(502) 583–8222

Other Books of Interest
from Servant Publications

The Greatest Counselor in the World
A Fresh, New Look at the Holy Spirit
Lloyd John Ogilvie

Christians face problems just like everyone else. The vital difference is that they have immediate and free access to a counselor who never makes a mistake and who has the power to help them cope and even change for the better.

Lloyd Ogilvie shows Christians how this divine counselor can lead them to the truth about themselves, grant them wisdom beyond their years, and fashion them into the likeness of Christ. *$16.99*

Delighting God
How to Live at the Center of God's Will
D. James Kennedy

D. James Kennedy knows that it is only God who can satisfy our longing, calm our restlessness, and fill our emptiness with his tremendous love. Once we know that, we can begin to seek his will in earnest. We can enjoy an intimate relationship with God. We can know what it means to fall in love with the One who made us.

Delighting God is a book about the most important relationship anyone will ever have. It will help us to receive God's blessings and grow in our understanding of his loving plan for our lives. *$8.99*

Available at your local Christian bookstore or from:
Servant Publications • Dept. 209 • P.O. Box 7455
Ann Arbor, Michigan 48107
Please include payment plus $2.75 per book
for postage and handling.
*Send for our FREE catalog of Christian
books, music, and cassettes.*